Digging
Deeper

Digging Deeper

Understanding how your garden works

Paul Williams

To my Mum and Dad

First published in 2002 by
Conran Octopus Limited
A part of Octopus Publishing Group
2–4 Heron Quays
London E14 4JP

www.conran-octopus.co.uk

ISBN 1 84091 267 7

British Library Cataloguing-in-Publication Data
A catalogue record for this book is available from the British Library

Printed and bound in China

Publishing Director: Lorraine Dickey
Senior Editor: Katey Day
Managing Editor: Helen Ridge

Creative Director: Leslie Harrington
Art Editor: Mary Staples
Picture Researcher: Liz Boyd

Senior Production Controller: Manjit Sihra

Contents

6 *Introduction*

8 *Let's get physical*
The structure and mechanics of plants

34 *Surviving the seasons*
How plants adapt to the seasons

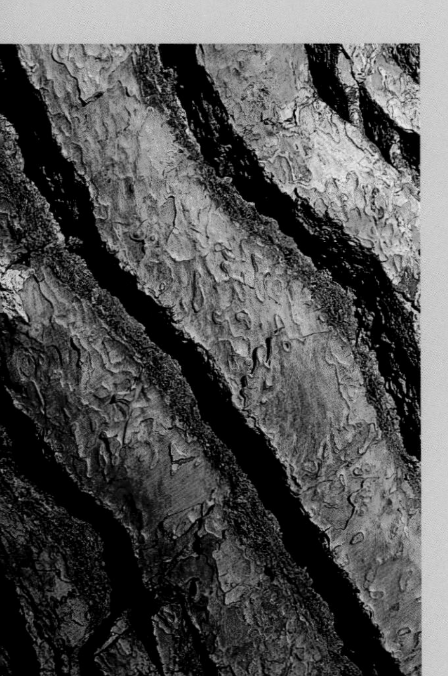

46 *Plumbing the depths*
What roots do

56 *All things bright and beautiful*
Colour and scent

68 *Getting a grip*
How plants support themselves

78 *Keeping the enemy at bay*
Dealing with pests and diseases

104 *Floral sex*
How plants propagate

126 *Dishing the dirt*
Appreciating the soil

146 *Name that plant*
Understanding scientific plant names

156 *Index*
160 *Acknowledgments*

Introduction

I hope that as you read this book you will be inspired to go outside and take a really close look at your garden. No matter how small, the garden is a place of intense activity, and you will get even more pleasure from it – and become a better gardener – if you understand what is taking place. Watch the insects visiting the flowers and carrying off the pollen; turn over the compost heap to see the worms eating their way through it; think about how water gets from root tip to tree top; and be amazed at the rate aphids multiply. Although it may sound clichéd, get a feeling for the way nature works – observation and understanding are everything. It doesn't matter whether you have a manicured garden with a wide range of plants or a rather scruffy-looking backyard with just a few hostas and a buddleja – there will still be something to excite you.

Take time to find out where your plants originate. Even if you have only a few plants, you'll probably discover that they are from various parts of the world: asters from the United States, bergenias from Siberia, wisterias from China and Japan, for example. This knowledge alone could lead you to compare climates and wonder what kind of habitat each plant enjoys in its native land. Perhaps you'll then try to emulate that environment in the garden so that your plants can reach their full potential.

There is beauty to be found not only in the plants that we introduce to our gardens but also in the unwelcome pests and diseases that come in of their own accord, perhaps tempted by the feast we have laid before them. Aphids, moulds, rusts and rots all have a beauty that, believe it or not, is well

Every garden is teeming with activity and life, some of it blatantly obvious like these buds bursting in spring but much of it going on unnoticed in the roots, shoots and leaves. The vital processes of nourishment, of energy gathering, of food transport, of procreation, are all hidden and mostly unthought of but awesome in their complexity and ingenuity.

worth appreciating before we reach for the sprayer. In addition, many of these pests and diseases have complex life cycles that involve a variety of hosts, and many produce different types of adult or types of spore for a range of conditions.

Every plant has a scientific name and, although these names may sound daunting, trying to understand them will lead you down intriguing paths of discovery. They may tell you where the plant came from originally, who introduced it, what it looks like, what growing conditions it prefers, and even some obscure but fascinating information that will help build the character of the plant.

This book is not intended to provide every answer to your gardening questions but I hope that it will set you off on a trail of exploration and understanding. It should encourage you to see the garden as a complex living entity where the pleasure comes not just from the brightly coloured flowers but also from an understanding of the relationships between all its different elements.

As a final tip in this introduction, I should like to recommend that you always carry a small hand lens in your pocket when out and about in the garden. Even the most mundane-looking leaf, twig or bug takes on a new dimension when seen through a x10 lens (ask your local jeweller where you can buy one). Although there are features and devices to thrill and enthral with the naked eye, the enjoyment and amazement to be had from seeing things close up is an experience that takes some beating and the excitement never diminishes, no matter how often you do it.

Let's get physical

Back to basics

Plants can be broken down into several basic parts, with each one a vital component in a production line. When everything is running smoothly, healthy plants are the result.

The most exciting aspect of foliage is its variety in both shape and colour. But closer inspection reveals even more intricate variation in the arrangement of the leaf veins. This *Phormium tenax* has veins that run almost parallel along the length of the leaf blade. Other leaves are covered in an intricate dividing network of veins spreading from a central rib.

Understanding how the whole factory operates and how it uses its raw materials allows us better to control the end product more effectively. By knowing the way in which a leaf works, for example, you'll realize just how important it is to supply a plant with the conditions it needs. Learning the internal mechanisms of a plant will give you a whole new insight into traditional gardening techniques.

LOOKING AT THE LEAF

It is easy to take leaves for granted. They unfurl in the spring, sit there during the summer, become a bit tatty as autumn approaches and they might produce a final burst of fiery colour before they finally fall to the ground in winter. What we don't see is the myriad of processes going on, from the moment they open out and turn to the light to the time their lives end.

Its purpose in life

A leaf's job is to gather light energy to power food production in the plant. This rather bland statement of fact gives little idea of just where the leaf and its processes stand in relation to the wellbeing of not just your garden but the whole planet. The leaf and its processes are the very crux of life. Leaves maintain our atmosphere by replenishing the oxygen used up by animals and man and, with the energy they produce, they sustain the world's food production as well as supporting the whole animal kingdom. Less important on a world scale but closer to home for the gardener, they also provide a palette of colours, shapes and textures that at times seems limitless.

If you look around the garden at the wide variety of leaves, you might think that the term 'a typical leaf' is rather meaningless but, despite the differences in shape, colour and texture, the majority of leaves have a similar structure. So, although leaves vary greatly in size and shape, they are typically flat and thin. This gives them the greatest surface area for light gathering, together with the minimum volume, so that air and light can easily penetrate all parts of the leaf.

On the upper surface of a leaf there is a protective 'skin', which you can see on the leaves of certain plants – a good example is the succulent *Echeveria*. If you bend and snap an *Echeveria* leaf, then peel it back on itself, the thin skin will lift from the leaf. This skin becomes obvious on the leaves of other plants that have been attacked by leaf miners; these insects eat the inside of the leaf, leaving the outer skin intact. This skin helps protect the leaf from physical damage and pests as well as preventing water loss. Below it are upright layers of long cells called

palisade cells, which are designed to carry light right down into the leaf. Their contents are virtually clear and each layer of palisade cells traps some of the light as it passes through the leaf.

Making food

Each leaf is like a small factory that uses water, carbon dioxide and the sun's energy – three fairly nebulous elements – to produce food for the plant in the form of sugars. This process, which is called photosynthesis, is capable of turning a tiny seedling into a 110m (360ft) high tree weighing hundreds of tonnes.

Scattered within leaf cells are tiny structures called chloroplasts (from the Greek *chloros*, meaning green, and *plastos*, meaning body), and within these is a pigment called chlorophyll (from *phyll*, meaning leaf). Chlorophyll absorbs red and blue light but reflects green and that is why we see leaves as green. There are other pigments present but for most of the year they are masked by the chlorophyll (see page 62). Some leaves are not green at all – look at *Ophiopogon planiscapus* 'Nigrescens'. This is as black a plant as you can imagine, suggesting that there is no chlorophyll present, but as plants cannot live without chlorophyll, you know that it is simply masked by other pigments.

Nitrogen is a key component of chlorophyll molecules and very important for healthy plants. When plants are short of nitrogen, which is one of the nutrients most readily leached from the soil, they become pale green. The effect can most obviously be seen on a poorly growing lawn that has not been fertilized for a long time. If the lawn is given a high nitrogen feed, the grass will turn a rich dark green and start growing much faster – and need cutting more often!

Chlorophyll takes light energy from the sun and creates an electric current that is used to split water into its two elements: hydrogen and oxygen. The hydrogen in the plant combines with the carbon and oxygen from carbon dioxide in the air to produce sugars, with excess oxygen released back into the atmosphere for us to breathe. (Commercial growers enrich the atmosphere of their greenhouses with extra carbon dioxide to increase the growth rates of plants.)

For photosynthesis to take place there has to be a supply of water and carbon dioxide within the leaf. Water is transported up from the roots through tubes in the stem, out into side branches and into the leaf where it is distributed, usually via a main rib or ribs, to a network of ever-dividing veins. Any one of these veins can be traced back as a continuous tube right down to the root tips. Apart from supplying water and nutrients to the leaf, the thickened veins and midrib also give the leaf structural strength.

Fortunately for the gardener, this major functional structure can be used to great ornamental effect, enriching the garden with texture and pattern. The large and dramatic leaves of *Gunnera manicata* show how valuable the effect of deep-set veins can be, as do the palmate leaves of another moisture-loving plant

Top right Plants that grow in the shade often have a higher concentration of chlorophyll to make the most of what light is available. Others, like this hosta, have very broad leaves to catch as much light as possible and give them a competitive edge.

Bottom right The prominent veins on ruby chard are a striking feature of the plant but, apart from their obvious ornamental value, they make it easy to see how veins divide and re-divide to ensure that all parts of the leaf receive water and nutrients.

Rodgersia podophylla. The tender perennial *Ricinus communis* 'Gibsonii' produces a gorgeous effect with red veins across a bronzed green leaf. The arrangement of veins on the large though otherwise ordinary leaves of *Hosta sieboldiana* var. *elegans* turns the leaves into ribbed and puckered paddles. On a much smaller scale the shiny leaves of ground-covering *Ajuga reptans* 'Atropurpurea' and the softly ribbed *Alchemilla mollis* are both enhanced by the pattern of their veins.

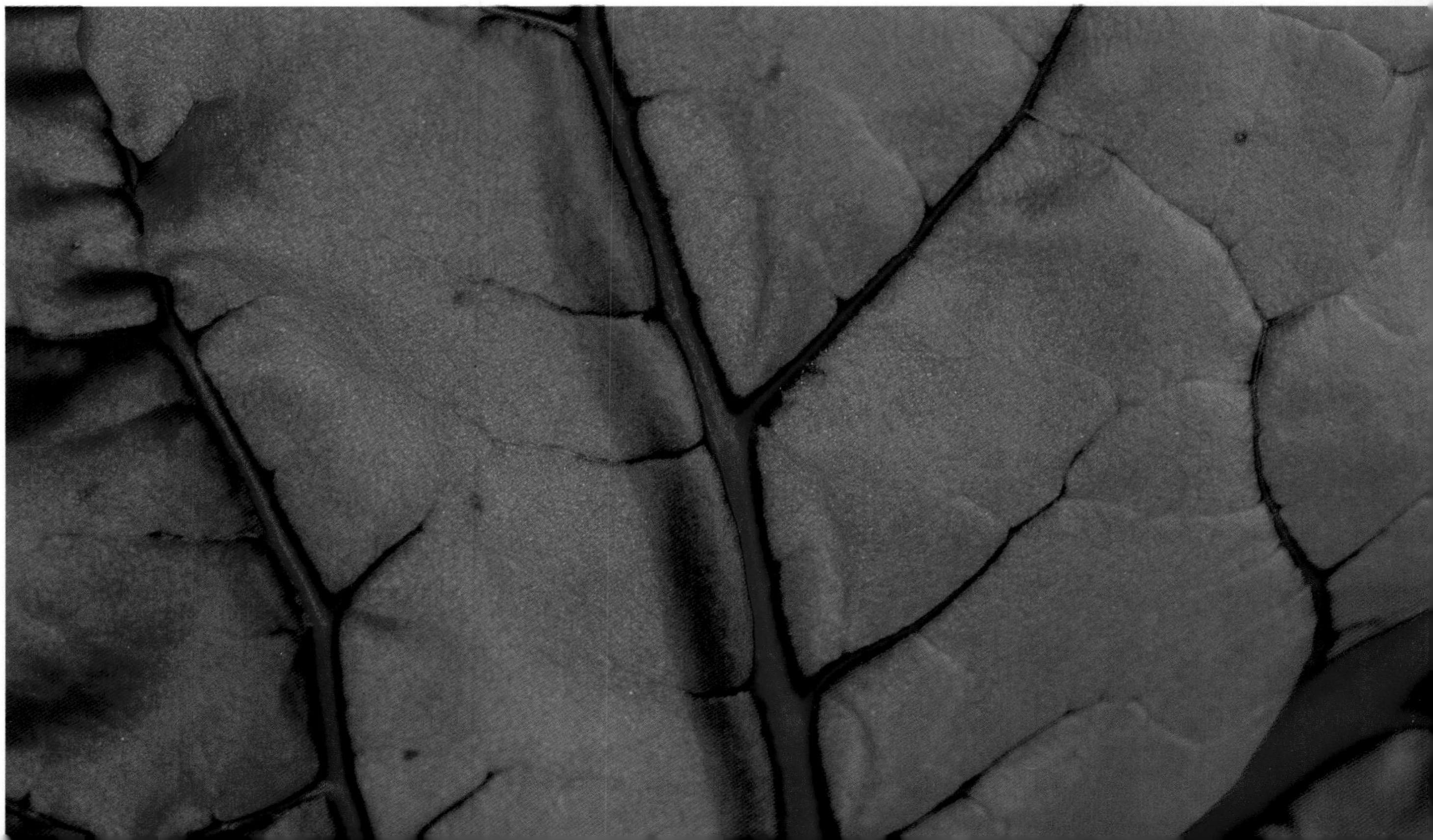

Carbon dioxide enters the plant as a constituent of air. It enters through tiny pores called stomata (from the Greek *stoma*, meaning mouth). These are usually on the underside of the leaf so that they stay clean and are less susceptible to attack by fungal spores, which are more likely to settle on the upper surface of the leaf. However, the stomata of plants like the water lily

have to be on the upper surface, and on grassy leaves, which do not really have an upper and lower surface, they are more evenly distributed on both sides.

These pores, visible with a low-powered microscope, are surrounded by two sausage-like cells. When the two cells are 'relaxed', they straighten out and sit tight together, closing off the pore; when they are filled with water pressure they regain their sausage shape, creating an oval opening between them to allow air to pass in and out of the leaf. The stomata are so tiny that it is hard to imagine that, on a sunny day, they let in sufficient air to supply the process of photosynthesis, but when we see how many of them there are it is easier to understand. Numbers range from about 45,000 per square centimetre on the under surface of an orange leaf to 25,000 on lilac leaves and 10,000 on holly leaves. Why there is such a difference in the number of stomata on the leaves of different species may have more to do with the environment and temperature that these plants grow in rather than a greater or lesser need to photosynthesize (see page 38).

Harsh environments force some drastic adaptations on to plants. These rounded *Mammillaria* cacti show a whole range of solutions to help conserve moisture and stay cool in hot, dry conditions. They are low growing to reduce the effect of drying winds, rounded for minimum surface area, covered in heat-reflecting and moisture-trapping hairs and clustered together for mutual protection.

Leaf shapes and modifications

Some leaves have become so modified after millions of years of evolution that they are barely recognizable as such. An obvious example is the cactus. Driven by its need to conserve water and withstand the rigours of a hot and dry climate, the leaves have become nothing more than spines with the function of photosynthesis taken over by the fleshy stem. On climbing plants like the grape vine, some of the leaves have developed into tendrils. The complex 'traps' of insectivorous plants are a particularly dramatic development. It is hard to conceive that these started off as leaves and have gradually turned into very elaborate structures, some with a reservoir of digesting juice, others with sticky hairs and hinged traps ready to snap over unsuspecting insects that touch the trigger hairs. What makes them more interesting is that they have taken on part of the root's job. They trap insects to provide the plant with nitrogen, which is usually gathered by the roots, but in areas where the soil contains little nitrogen, it has to be supplemented through these modified leaves.

Surprising developments

Some leaves make visible rapid movements. You may have touched the leaves of the sensitive plant (*Mimosa pudica*) to see how they collapse and noticed that the collapse often spreads beyond the leaves touched, suggesting that a chemical message is being sent through the plant. In this extreme case, the cells can become pressurized or deflated very quickly, causing the 'hinged' part of the plant to move one way or another. Several plants show similar but slower, less dramatic movement, including species of *Oxalis* and clover, which close their leaves at night or in times of stress, such as great heat or drought.

Leaves provide other unexpected surprises. Those of the pick-a-back plant (*Tolmiea menziesii*), a hardy groundcover plant often treated as a house plant, produce new plants from the point where the leaf stalk joins the leaf blade; these eventually root into the soil, thereby spreading the plant. The fleshy Mexican hat plant (*Kalanchoe daigremontiana*) produces rows of small plants along its leaf edges that fall to the ground and put down roots.

One explanation for these unusual growths is that when the very young leaf, buried under the surface of the stem, starts to develop, the bud just above it, which usually stays on the stem, gets carried out with the growing leaf. This then gives it the potential to produce unexpected effects. Another possible cause is that before the leaves start developing they are just a group of very young cells that have not differentiated, and so they are all capable of producing young plants. As the leaf develops and the cells specialize, some of the cells with the ability to make new plants survive within the leaf and then later produce growth in unexpected places.

Some leaves develop structures called extrafloral nectaries (extra in the sense of outside or apart from – think extramarital affair). These nectaries are produced outside their normal position in the flower and, like the genuine article, produce nectar. Take a look at the leaf blade of the guelder rose (*Viburnum opulus*) where it joins the stalk and you can easily see the small knobbly glands that produce nectar. Passionflowers (*Passiflora*) have them in the same position but they are less obvious. The purpose of these nectaries is not always clear but it seems to be tied up with attracting insects, particularly ants and parasitic wasps, that will help defend the plant against other pests more likely to eat it.

Sometimes we can only guess at what reason lies behind a particular leaf shape. But even if we do not understand the purpose of its design, we can still marvel at the neatness and charm of the arrangement of leaf and flower on plants like this *Montia perfoliata.*

Let there be light

Receiving sufficient light is the essence of a plant's existence, so it is not surprising that there are mechanisms to ensure that its leaves get enough. If you leave seedlings in the dark for too long or try to eradicate weeds by covering them with black polythene, you will see pale plants with elongated stems struggling towards the light. If your seedlings do not get light, they will quickly exhaust their store of food and die, which is exactly what you are hoping will happen to the weeds you have covered in the garden. However, some of these will have big reserves of energy and take up to a season or more to become exhausted. Bindweed is such a plant – its thick fleshy roots store enough energy to keep the plant alive without light for a whole season.

Both seedlings and weeds bend their stems towards any chink of light, as do some plants growing in the shade. This happens because growth hormones called auxins move from the lighter to the darker side of the stem, where they cause more rapid growth, thereby pushing the stem over towards the light.

Generally low light levels stimulate the activation of another growth hormone that causes the internodes (the part of the stem between the leaf joints) to elongate. It is a combination of these two responses that cause shrubs growing close to walls or in shady spots to lean out to the light and grow in a distorted or lopsided fashion. It is better to choose a suitable shade-tolerant shrub or perennial than to endure a poorly shaped plant that is only spoiled by continual tying back or pruning in an effort to make it look acceptable. Plants that are happy to grow in the shade have developed the ability to photosynthesize and thrive in low light conditions without growing leggy stems.

Commercial house-plant growers manipulate growth by applying chemicals to control the hormones that dictate the length of the stem and so produce a plant that is compact and neat and, of course, very saleable. However, if you keep this plant – let's say it's a pot chrysanthemum – for another season, you will find the effect of the chemical has worn off and what you thought was a dwarf plant will grow much bigger than you expected.

THE ROLE OF THE STEM

The stem has two main purposes: to get the leaves of the plant up to where they can reach sunlight and the flowers to where they can best be pollinated. The other is to support the tubes and vessels that move nutrients and water between the roots and leaves.

As with every other part of a plant, modifications and adaptations have led to a great variety of stem types, many of them barely recognizable as stems but nearly all represented in the average garden. There are underground stems, stems that run along the surface, stems that climb to many metres, stems that store food, stems as tough as rope, stems as fragile as a strand of hair, stems that last for less than a year and others that persist for several thousand years. Each has adapted to or exploited a set of environmental conditions that they have tried to make their own.

The cells in a stem originate from the growing tip of a shoot. This area of dividing cells is called the apical meristem. It is significant in several ways for gardeners. Because it is the intent of a plant to get its leaves up towards the light, the topmost growing tip takes priority over buds and sideshoots below it (this is called apical dominance). Growth regulators produced by the plant favour tip growth by inhibiting the growth of buds lower down. It is an effect that can be overcome by causing the redistribution of growth regulators. By bending branches or stems over so that they lie horizontally, the tip is no longer dominant and otherwise dormant buds along the length of the stem will start to grow. Gardeners have taken advantage of this technique for a long time by growing fruit as horizontal espaliers. This encourages the production of shoots and fruits along a horizontal branch, making a more compact and accessible plant.

The dominance of the leading shoot can be a nuisance to the gardener, particularly in the case of climbing roses, which, in response to their natural inclinations, send out long shoots that produce leaves and flowers only at the very top, leaving bare 'legs' below. They can be encouraged to flower along their length if the dominance of the shoot top is overcome by bending and tying down the shoots to as near horizontal as possible. Old shoots are almost impossible to bend, so start training young shoots early on. Cut out old stems and train in replacement shoots regularly.

We are unwittingly breaking this apical dominance when, in our efforts to produce a bushy plant, we prune or pinch out the growing tips. This removes the chemical that suppresses the growth of the lower buds, allowing the

By training fruit trees as espaliers and cordons we are unwittingly manipulating the concentrations of growth regulators within the stem. The continual pruning back and restriction of the top growth of plants also has the effect of reducing root growth.

Young shoots of shrubs and trees are pliant and soft but become stiffer and stronger as they mature, to support the ever-increasing weight of branches and leaves. Although they are purely functional, many branches and stems, like this *Cornus alba* 'Sibirica', are also colourful and can be used to good effect for winter display.

development of sideshoots and ultimately a fuller, bushier plant. This technique works on a wide range of plants and it is well worth trying on some leggy varieties of herbaceous perennials to produce a stockier plant that has no need of staking and tying, although this will cause them to flower a little bit later. For example, when tall phlox and asters reach a height of approximately 30cm (12in), pinch out the tips and you'll be amazed at the results – and you'll also be prolonging the flowering season.

To simplify our understanding of the growing stem, let's first break down stems into two types: herbaceous and woody.

Herbaceous stems

These are relatively soft, contain little woody material and are not designed to last season upon season. These are the stems of the herbaceous perennial, which dies down during the dormant season then grows up again the following year and reaches full height within a season. Herbaceous perennials are often simply referred to as perennials, which is a little misleading since perennial means 'lasting several years' and can apply equally to shrubs, trees and herbaceous plants.

In a herbaceous stem there are bundles of specialist cells that run the length of the stem and move water and nutrients around the plant. You may remember from your school days that these are called phloem and xylem tissues. Put simply, the xylem carries water and nutrients up from the roots to the leaves, and the phloem carries food generated in the leaves back around the plant. They run the length of the stem and into all branches and leaves (see also page 20). You might find it simpler to visualize these tubes within the plant as long drinking straws bound together and arranged as pairs. In each pair the 'straw' nearest the middle of the stem (the xylem) carries water up from the roots. It contains a bundle of continuous tubes made from long cells where the end walls have disappeared. They divide and run into all branches and leaves. The outer, usually much smaller straw (the phloem) carries bundles of long cells that have sieve-like ends through which pass the sugars manufactured in the leaves. Associated with these drinking straws are tough fibres that, along with the softer tissues, give the stem the resilience and pliability to withstand buffeting by the wind. Anyone who has chewed on a stick of rhubarb will undoubtedly have come across these stringy fibres, as will those who have worn linen that is made from the fibres of the flax plant. Try tearing across or cutting the leaf of a *Phormium* with anything less than sharp secateurs and you will appreciate their strength.

Woody stems

The second main type of stem is the woody stem. These make up the tough stems, branches and trunks of shrubs and trees. They form a rigid framework that is extended at the tips year by year and may take many years to reach its full extent. Growth can be slow as in plants that have adapted to, say, alpine or drought conditions, or very quick as in *Wisteria*, which is capable of making several metres of growth in a year (see also below). Woody stems get longer only from the tip, and because mature cells do not elongate, stems and branches older than one year will only get thicker not longer. This means that if you plant a standard tree such as a bay (standard is the term for a tree on a straight clear stem), the stem will not get any longer, it can only get thicker. Any extra height you want will have to be gained by allowing new shoots to grow upwards from the head of the tree.

In a woody stem the conducting cells, the xylem and the phloem, form concentric rings around the outside of the stem, much like the writing in a stick of rock, with the thinner phloem layer nearest the outer surface of the stem. Between these circular layers – imagine a tube within a tube – is a third layer. This is called the cambium layer (see also page 20), which is very active, generating new cells both on its inner – xylem – side and its outer – phloem – side. It is the cambium layer that produces the callousing you see on the end of cuttings before they root. It also forms the smooth rounded tissue that forms across the cut when a branch has been removed, and helps heal the wounds caused by lawnmower or strimmer damage to tree trunks (see page 24).

Stem shapes

A cylinder allows the maximum volume within the smallest external surface area, so it stands to reason that the majority of stems are more or less cylindrical. Some may be ridged, grooved or winged for extra strength. The woodier and more mature a stem becomes, the more likely it is to be cylindrical. Some young or herbaceous stems may be square, which can be useful when identifying a plant. Many good garden plants, such as sages (*Salvia*), ornamental deadnettles (*Lamium*), mints (*Mentha*), catmints (*Nepeta*), rosemary (*Rosmarinus*), *Phlomis*, *Teucrium* and *Ajuga*, have square stems.

Most woody stems are solid. Other smaller herbaceous plants have hollow stems and bearing in mind that their maximum height is reached in a single season, grow to considerable proportions. Consider the poisonous but majestic giant hogweed (*Heracleum mantegazzianum*). In a single season it sends up hollow stems 3m (10ft) high and strong enough to bear great cartwheel heads of flowers. There is the Himalayan balsam (*Impatiens glandulifera*), a potentially invasive annual plant with explosive seed pods that fling seeds far and wide, so be wary of introducing it to your garden. This plant rises from a seed to become a mature plant 2m (6½ft) high in just a few months. It has a very stout hollow stem, which can be a bulky 10cm (4in) across at its base. Plants like this leave me in awe of the way in which nature generates such an amount of plant material in so short a time and then has it collapse and die at the end of the season.

Plant design is a structural engineer's delight. Fast-growing stems of tall annuals, perennials and biennials, like this giant hogweed *Heracleum mantegazzianum*, have to be light, strong and cheap in energy terms to produce. They are in effect throw-away items once the plant has dispersed its seed.

It is hard to believe that plants like this *Chimonobambusa* bamboo are not simply there for our enjoyment. The superb beauty and elegance of these stems belie their purely functional role. Bamboos are among the tallest members of the grass family with the stems of some species reaching 30m (100ft), which is amazing in itself considering that they are hollow.

Bamboo stems are another wonder of structural design, as well as being one of the fastest growers – tropical species can grow a metre in 24 hours. The larger bamboos at 25–30m (80–100ft) high are proof of the strength of plant tissue and the robustness of the tube as a structural shape. They are tough members of the grass family with hollow stems joined across at the leaf nodes for extra strength. With none of the woody material associated with trees, they rely on bundles of tough fibres spaced throughout the stem for structural support – you can see these if you cut through a bamboo garden cane with sharp secateurs.

BARK

This is a general term often used to mean just the outer visible layer of the tree trunk, but it also applies to the several layers underneath that circle the outside of the stem of a woody plant. It is these layers that are crucial to a tree's survival. So vast is the variation in the plant kingdom that trying to describe a typical bark is fraught with difficulties and contradictions, but most woody plants show an arrangement as described below.

Find a thickish tree branch, about 2.5cm (1in) across, and saw through it. If you look at the cross section, you will see the annual growth rings showing how much the branch or trunk has 'thickened' each year. In larger trunks these are obvious but in smaller branches you may need a hand lens to see them. They are more obvious in some woods than others; for example, it is difficult to see growth rings in holly, a fine-grained wood, but relatively easy in hazel.

Around the very edge of the branch you will see the bark. If you are looking at fresh wood in spring and early summer when growth is active, you can peel the bark away quite easily. When you do this, the surface of the wood underneath will feel slimy. This sliminess is a thin layer of cells called the cambium layer (*cambium* is Latin for barrier), which sheathes the woody interior of the stem like a cylinder. On the inside this cambium layer makes new cells called xylem cells, which form the vessels that transport water up from the roots and are also the 'wood' of the plant; these are obviously important for the rigidity of the branch. On the outside the cambium layer makes phloem cells, which transport all the sugars and food produced by the leaves to the rest of the plant. More cells are produced on the inside of the cambium layer than on the outside, hence there are more wood cells than sugar transport cells. The ring of cambium also produces cells sideways to cover the growing circumference of wood it has produced on its inside. The combined production of these cells causes the stem to thicken each year. You will also be able to see lines or 'rays' of cells radiating from the centre of the branch, which transport water and food radially within the stem.

In spring plant growth is rapid and cells produced in the stem are large. As the season progresses and growth gradually slows down, the cells produced become smaller. If you cut through a tree trunk, you can easily see the contrast between

each season's large and small cells as concentric rings, and by counting them you can find out how old the tree is. To prevent you having to cut down a tree just to get an idea of its age, there is a rough rule of thumb that involves causing no physical harm to the tree. Every 2.5cm (1in) of girth measured at 1.5m (5ft) – about chest height – represents a year. Bear in mind, though, that this is a very general rule and that trees growing under difficult conditions, where light or water are restricted, for example, will not make typical growth and may not conform to this ratio.

Looking at a cross section of a stem it is hard to believe that the very narrow ring between the wood and the outer bark is sufficient to carry all the plant's nutrients around the tree and down to the roots. In a tree trunk 30cm (12in) across, only the outer 1cm (½in) is likely to be alive and active. Most of the internal wood is dead and simply provides structural support and a storage place for the plant's waste products. A graphic illustration of this outer 'cylinder' of living tissue is the number of old trees still growing despite the fact that their centres have long since rotted away, leaving a hollow trunk.

Above All living cells need oxygen and the only way a cell buried deep in a tree trunk has access to air is through lines of loosely packed cells radiating through the trunk and opening in the bark. *Prunus serrula*, along with other members of the cherry family, shows these cells quite clearly.

Far right As a tree expands the outer layer of bark is replaced from underneath with a new layer. Some shed this old bark in papery sheets giving the trunks an ornamental finish. In cold climates layers of peeling bark can form useful insulation. This is the bark of *Acer griseum*.

Since the tubes that transport nutrients around the tree are very near to the surface and therefore quite vulnerable, there is another layer, or cylinder, of cells around the stem sheathing these conducting tissues. This layer is also a sort of cambium and produces cork cells on its outside; this is the 'bark' that we see and that gives many trees their characteristic look. The main function of the outer bark is to provide a physical barrier to protect the tree from fungal and insect attack as well as keeping moisture both in and out. Some barks produce resins and latex that clog up the mouth parts of insects, while others produce unpalatable tannins (see page 84).

Designing with bark

Bark is also a source of inspiration when creating a garden. Colours range from the blindingly white bark of some of birches, such as *Betula utilis* var. *jacquemontii*, to reds (*Cornus alba* 'Sibirica', *Acer palmatum* 'Sango-kaku'), greens

(*Kerria japonica*) and warm coppery browns (*Prunus maackii*). To complement this variety of colour there is a wide range of textures. Birches and cherries offer silky smooth barks, some so smooth that they shine. (The story goes that in years gone by young gardeners on large estates were required to buff up the shiny bark of *Prunus serrula* to give it that extra gleam.) The sweet chestnut (*Castanea sativa*) has a deeply fissured and twisted bark, the Wellingtonia (*Sequoiadendron giganteum*) a ruddy coloured fibrous bark soft enough to punch without hurting your hand, and the strawberry tree (*Arbutus unedo*) an ornamental bark that shreds in irregular and curling oblong pieces. The paperbark maple (*Acer griseum*) and the river birch (*Betula nigra*) both have peeling papery shaggy barks. *Euonymus alatus* sheds its brilliantly coloured autumn leaves to reveal prominent corky wings on its branches, while the large eucalyptus family alone has an outstanding range of colours and textures. These qualities and the fact that bark is one of the most noticeable features in winter make it an important consideration when putting together plant combinations for year-round effect.

Adapting to the environment

Evolution has guided plant development down many paths and no less so than with the formation of barks. Environmental pressures, some not always obvious, others perhaps no longer relevant, have given rise to a very wide range of bark types to cope with different conditions.

In dry regions some trees have no leaves for several months as a way of conserving water, but in order to take over part of the job of making energy that the absent leaves would ordinarily carry out, the bark has become green and photosynthetic. Many eucalyptus trees have green, photosynthetic bark, which is constantly being exposed as layers of old bark peel away. The strawberry tree (*Arbutus unedo*) also reveals green bark under its outer peeling bark.

In several regions of the world it is natural for forest fires to burn through at regular intervals, and many forest trees have developed fire-resistant barks, to help insulate them from the intense heat. Some of these trees can make attractive additions to a large garden, and include the Douglas fir (*Pseudotsuga menziesii*), Wellingtonia (*Sequoiadendron giganteum*) and the giant redwood (*Sequoia sempervirens*).

Bark is produced in varying thicknesses and patterns. Certain species of birch produce barks that are almost as thin as paper. The most obvious example of a thick bark is that of the cork oak (*Quercus suber*), whose bark is used for the commercial production of wine corks and other cork products. The thick layer of cork on the cork oak and other thick-barked trees may have cell walls impregnated with suberin, a fatty substance impermeable to gases and water. Cork tissue is produced as live cells but they eventually die to form a protective layer. Some may slough off to be replaced by new cells from beneath.

As the circumference of a tree gets bigger, cracks may appear in the bark to make allowance for the greater girth beneath, or it might peel away or be shed in irregular plates as new layers of bark form underneath.

All plant cells, whether they are in the roots or the shoots, need oxygen. To make sure that cells in the trunk and branches of a tree get sufficient oxygen, the plant has lines of open-spaced cells that erupt through the bark in features called lenticels. These appear as rough lines running either around or along the length of the trunk and branches. They are very obvious running around the trunk and branches of birches and many types of ornamental and fruiting cherries, and they stand out clearly on the branches of elderberry (*Sambucus nigra*), and give them a very rough look. The bark of the cork oak is particularly thick and impervious to air, and without the lenticels the essential gas exchange between the inner cells and the atmosphere could not take place. To ensure an efficient movement of gases the lines of lenticels through the cork are large and therefore quite noticeable. Next time you open a bottle of wine, take a look at the cork: you can often see the lenticels as dark lines running across a cork made from a single piece of bark. On other types of trees and shrubs the lenticels look like random speckles.

Now and then you may come across trees that have a considerable bulge in the bark just above or below a distinct line around the trunk. This is often seen on old cherry trees and usually occurs just below the crown or just above ground level. It is the result of two varieties of cherry with different growth rates grafted together, with one thickening up more quickly than the other. The position of the bulge depends on whether they were grafted at the top of the stem or near the ground. Some compatible varieties have the same growth rate but different bark patterns, and you occasionally see mature trees with two dissimilar barks separated by what remains a surprisingly distinct and straight graft line.

Shrubs tied to a wall or post with wire can show a similar effect when the wire is left on too long. The efforts of the plant to move water and nutrients up and down the stem past the restriction cause a bulge of tissue. This throttling reduces the upward flow of water, resulting in poor growth above the wire. Regular checking of ties and the use of string that eventually rots will prevent this potentially lethal problem.

As we have seen, the vital conducting cells that allow movement of water and food around the plant are just under the bark, so it is vital when using a strimmer to keep it away from the trunks of young trees and shrubs that have not developed a sufficiently thick protective bark. A strimmer can flail the complete circumference of a young trunk and strip off the essential layers of cells, guaranteeing its death. Gouging pieces out of the trunk by getting too close with a lawnmower can also have disastrous results, not just by reducing the plant's capacity to move nutrients about but also by removing the protective coating of bark and allowing fungal disease and water to enter.

WHAT MAKES A STEM A STEM?

We tend to think of stems as upright structures that carry leaves and flowers, but nature, being the inventive and adaptable force it is, has caused some stems to grow not quite as we might expect. A closer look reveals that there are parts of plants familiar to the gardener that are, in fact, stems, although we never think of them as such. These stems have been given specific names, some of which you probably already know, for example, rhizome, corm and tuber. But, you may ask, if they don't look like stems, how do we know they are stems? What is it exactly that makes a stem a stem?

The stems that we are familiar with have nodes – the points from which the leaves arise – and they almost always have a bud in the joint between the stem and leaf – this is called an axillary bud. The length of stem between two nodes is called the internode and can vary in length; in some plants the internodes are so short that they look nothing like a stem at all. So, to qualify as a stem there must be leaves and axillary buds present.

Many irises produce vigorous rhizomes. The rhizomes of *Iris pseudacorus* form large dense colonizing mats in moist or wet conditions, binding the soil. The variegated form is slightly less vigorous and makes a handsome garden plant for soils that do not dry out.

Rhizomes

An underground stem that grows more or less horizontally is called a rhizome. They are often thick and fleshy but not always. There are plenty of examples among garden plants, such as ornamental gingers (*Hedychium*), Solomon's seal (*Polygonatum multiflorum)* and bearded irises. The iris is a good example to study in the garden because in older clumps the rhizomes are likely to be on the surface. Close inspection of the horizontal rhizome will show closely packed lines that are the scars where old leaves were attached, proving that it is a stem. You may also notice a dotting of root scars near the undersurface of the rhizome. The newer leaves are at the tip of the stem. Houseplant rhizomes include the small and insignificant-looking scaled rhizomes of the hot water plant (*Achimenes*) and the evergreen sedge *Cyperus involucratus*.

There are far less desirable and very persistent rhizomes that cause heartache in many a garden. The grass *Agropyron repens*, with its string of familiar common names including couch grass, twitch and squitch, has vigorous and far-reaching thin underground stems. Dig up a piece and you will see the long rhizomes spreading through the soil. The tip of each horizontal rhizome is tough and needle-like to help it forge through the ground; I have dug up potatoes speared through by these sharp shoots, which have pierced the potato tuber and grown through and out the other side.

In open ground or under shrubs this pernicious grass can be controlled with the careful use of systemic weedkillers (see page 103), but once it finds its way into a clump of herbaceous perennials, chemicals cannot be used safely. Your choices then are to dig up and remove the perennial completely or to split it into small enough pieces so that the roots can be washed and every trace of the grass removed. A physical barrier going down 30cm (12in) into the soil and standing a few centimetres above it is the only way to stop couch grass invading your garden from your neighbour's.

New strawberry plants can be propagated from the plants that are formed at the end of the runners. They are likely to bear fruit the following year.

Right alongside couch grass in its ability to swamp borders and frustrate gardeners is *Aegopodium podagraria* – this, too, has a long list of common names including ground elder, bishop's weed (apparently monks used to eat it), herb Gerard and ground ash. It forms a matrix of rhizomes that also penetrates clumps of ornamentals, and these become a reservoir of shoots that will creep back out into the border no matter how often you clear the surrounding ground. These rhizomatous shoots can form roots and, by definition, are able to produce leaves, so any tiny pieces left in the garden, provided they have a node, will be able to form a new plant.

Stolons and runners

These are two types of stem with similar functions and arrangements. A stolon lies just under or on the surface of the ground whereas a runner is above the surface. Stolons carry leaves and are likely to root at each node. A common example in the garden is clover, often found in lawns because its low flat growth keeps it out of the way of the lawnmower blades. To slow down its spread without the use of chemicals it is worthwhile using the following technique before mowing. Rake the patch of clover with a spring rake to flick up the stolons so that they will be caught in the mower.

Runners do not root at every node and do not usually have leaves along their length even at the nodes, though there may be scale leaves present at this point. At the end of a runner a new plant will be formed, making roots and shoots. This, in turn, will produce runners to spread the plant still further. Strawberry plants behave in this way. If you look at the runners, you will see along their length a node and a tiny scale leaf, proving that they are stems. Also examine a house leek (*Sempervivum*) in your alpine trough – its 'offspring' are all formed at the end of runners.

Ornamental plants that spread by stolons or runners can be rather invasive in the garden, but this quality can also make them good groundcover and able to colonize ground unsuitable for other plants. *Persicaria affinis*, *Waldsteinia ternata*, some of the *Acaena* and *Ajuga reptans* are all attractive groundcover plants that spread by stolons or runners, usefully smothering lesser weeds and, at the same time, binding loose soil on banks and slopes.

Corms

There is something about corms that always makes me smile. Whether it is the fact that they are, in effect, squashed-down stems and their identity crisis shows through, or perhaps there is something intrinsically comical in their often dumpy rotund shape, I don't know.

Comical or not, they are remarkable pieces of plant material because what you are seeing is a very short stem. Take a look at a *Gladiolus* or crocus corm, or dig up a few corms of a *Crocosmia*. On the *Gladiolus* corm you can see the concentric rings that are the leaf scars from leaves shed at the end of the season.

Houseleeks (*Sempervivum*) are among the easiest of plants to grow. They colonize areas by putting out runners with a small plant at the tip.

The crocus has a similar arrangement. At the end of the season a crocus corm will be sheathed with scale leaves and withered foliage leaves. If these are peeled off, the concentric leaf scars can be seen. Each scar carries a bud, although they are often barely visible. Near the top of the corm there will be some better developed large buds. These large buds will form next year's corms. By the following spring they will have enlarged and be sending out foliage. The foliage will feed the new corm causing it to swell and become the stored food supply to see the plant over winter. As the new corms develop the old one withers and the process starts all over again. Where new corms are formed on top of the old one, it is easy to imagine the plants eventually coming out of the ground, but contractile roots pull the new corms back down into the ground.

The corms of the *Crocosmia* are a little different. They do not wither within one season and instead build up into bobbly strings of corms sheathed in the remains of old foliage and scale leaves. Strip off the old leaves and, with a hand lens, check out the shiny pinkish orange-peel-like surface of the corm. The *Crocosmia* also sends out rhizomes that put out new stems, that is, corms, to form new plants at a distance from the parent plant.

Other common garden plants that grow from corms include freesias, *Tigridia*, *Ixia*, *Gladiolus callianthus* and *Moraea*.

Tubers

The first two plants that come to mind when I think of tubers are potato and dahlia. Although both tubers are made to store energy, they are quite distinct from each other: the potato is a stem tuber, the dahlia a root tuber.

If you compare the two, you will see that the dahlia tuber is fairly uniform in shape and surface and its 'fleshy fingers' emanate from the base of the stem. In contrast, the potato is a swelling on an otherwise fairly thin 'root', which does, in fact, seem to be a part of the root system. While the potato itself is a fairly even shape, its surface has little dips called 'eyes' – if you haven't noticed these, then you obviously haven't peeled enough spuds. Each of these 'eyes' comprises a bud and a leaf scar, which we now know tells us that it is a stem. Because it is a stem, when it is planted it can use the energy stored in the tuber to make the buds grow and form new shoots and leaves. If you don't sort out your vegetable bin often enough, you will no doubt have experienced this happening in your own kitchen.

The potato will tolerate being cut into several pieces and, provided they have an 'eye', there is a good chance of each one growing into a new potato plant when planted. However, if you cut off a swollen dahlia root, it will never grow because it is a true root and has no capacity to produce shoots.

Another common tuberous stem is the Jerusalem artichoke (*Helianthus tuberosus*), a relative of the sunflower. If you have tried to get rid of a bed of this rather rampant yet ornamental vegetable, you will know that the smallest part left

in the ground will start a new plant. That is because the 'roots' are, in fact, stem tubers, with lots of buds just waiting to burst into life and reinvade your plot. A less invasive (at least in cooler climates) and far more attractive plant with an edible tuber is the orange-flowered climber *Tropaeolum tuberosum*. The tubers are yellowish and knobbly with flecks of red.

Tubers are full of stored energy, which makes them a rich food source for man but, unfortunately, also for pests like squirrels and mice, which will dig up newly planted tubers or help themselves to those being overwintered.

You wouldn't expect to find a swollen stem deep under the soil, but that is just what a potato tuber is, even though it looks exactly like a swollen root. The potato is easily propagated and a readily stored form of food energy, which contributes to its success as a very important food crop worldwide.

Cladodes

Butcher's broom (*Ruscus aculeatus*) is a curious garden plant, often found growing happily in deep shade (it gets its name supposedly because its tough and spiky nature made it a useful tool for cleaning butcher's blocks). Oddly, it appears to produce flowers in the middle of its leaves. A close-up inspection of one of the 'leaves' will show that in the middle there is a tiny bud. Just below it there is a small leaf scale, which tells us that what looks like a leaf is, in fact, a stem that has become flattened and taken on the food-manufacturing role of the leaf. This modified stem is called a cladode. Other plants with flattened stems include *Rhipsalidopsis rosea* and *Asparagus densiflorus*.

EFFECTIVE SELF-DEFENCE

Considering that plants are at the base of every food chain, it is hardly surprising that some of them have developed ways of protecting themselves. Arming leaves with spines or prickles is one very good way that a plant can prevent itself from becoming the meal of the next herbivore to come along. Prickles or thorns on the stem stop animals climbing the plant to feed on the leaves. As is usual in the natural world nothing is straightforward, so what might seem to be a means of protection, such as a thorn, may indeed be a feature the plant has developed to help it climb, as in the case of the rose or *Bougainvillea* (see page 75). These thorns obviously offer protection as well as a means of climbing, so there might be a chicken and egg question here. Did the thorns develop as protection then turn out to help the plant climb, or did they develop as climbing aids that happened to offer protection? When time travel is possible we might find out.

The thorns, or spines, of the cactus are another slightly ambiguous feature. They are leaves that, in an effort to reduce water loss from the plant, have become no more than tough sharp needles (see page 14). But here again they have the added benefit of protecting the precious water stored in the plant.

Some thorns are obviously for protection, as those who have ever pruned a firethorn (*Pyracantha*), hawthorn (*Crataegus*) or the ornamental gooseberry relative *Ribes speciosum* will know for sure. And anyone who has used their

The *Chorisia* from tropical America is ideally suited to preventing any animal scaling the trunk to feed on the foliage or fruit. Its hardened spines emerge from just under the bark and contain no vascular tissue. Appropriately, its common name is the anti-possum tree.

bare hands to gather fallen leaves within the vicinity of a holly bush or tried to uproot a thistle will also testify to the value of spines as a protective device.

Although most spines, prickles and stinging hairs have the same protective purpose, they originate from different parts of the plant. Prickles can be found arising on leaves, with holly being the obvious example, but there are some very efficient-looking prickles on the leaves of many species of *Solanum*, including the aubergine plant *Solanum melongena*. These prickles are outgrowths on or just under the leaf's skin, or epidermis. In the holly, by contrast, prickles are adaptations of the main leaf veins, which have hardened at the point where they come to the edge of the leaf.

Take a look at the thorns on a branch of *Pyracantha* and you will see that they arise from an axillary bud – that is the point where the leaf joins the stem – exactly as a shoot would do, which shows them to be modified stems. The growing tip of what would be the shoot has stopped producing new cells and has become woody. In fact, the long thorns often have leaves growing from them, further confirming their origins as stems. Hawthorns and blackthorn (*Prunus spinosa*) are also protected by stem thorns.

We know that the position of a leaf is usually just under a bud or shoot, so any feature that is not a leaf but is positioned just under a bud is likely to be a modified leaf. Looking at a branch of *Berberis julianae*, a most vicious and

effective plant for a boundary hedge, you can see that the spines occur just under a shoot, showing them to be a modified leaf. In this case, the stipule, too, has turned into a spine. Stipules are outgrowths associated with the base of a leaf. These are easily seen on most *Pelargonium* varieties, resembling a pair of small leaves either side of the leaf base.

Nettles and exotic plants like *Loasa* have more potent ways of protecting themselves. They develop sharp hair cells both on the stem and leaves. Each hair is a single cell that grows out into a point. The cells are hollow and filled with a poison under pressure so that when the sharp but brittle silicon tip is broken the poison is forced out into what ever has touched the plant, with the all too familiar reaction of swelling, irritation and soreness. Thistles also have formidable hair cells; they contain no poison but die and remain on the plant as hardened spines, protecting the plant from hungry herbivores.

Above From the plant's point of view spines and thorns offer protection and aid climbing, but for the gardener they are yet another feature that can be shown off in the garden. *Rosa sericea* subsp. *omeiensis* has some of the most dramatic and ornamental spines. For maximum effect plant it so that the sunlight will shine through the young thorns, and cut the plant back each year to promote new shoots because the older thorns become opaque.

Right If you have ever collected *Berberis* prunings without wearing stout gloves, you will know just how effective they are as a defence. A scattering of spiky prunings across your seed beds is a useful way to keep animals off. No matter how functional a plant's adaptations may be, there is always an element of beauty to be found, as with this *Berberis sieboldii*.

Above Cactus spines help protect the plant from animals intent on raiding the store of water held within the fleshy stem. In many cases the spines are barbed and come away from the plant once they pierce the skin, causing irritation.

Left *Gunnera manicata* has some of the largest leaves of all hardy plants. Their huge spread is supported by great ribs radiating from the top of a stout stem. The stem is made unattractive to animals by a covering of stiff spines, which add to the plant's rather threatening character.

Surviving

the seasons

Some like it hot

A leaf is a leaf is a leaf, right? Well, yes and no. All leaves are there to serve the same purpose, that is to gather light energy to power food production (see page 10), but a quick look around the garden will show that there is no such thing as a 'standard' leaf.

Compare the narrow downy leaves of lavender with the broad smooth blades of hostas, the grassy leaves of *Iris sibirica* with the glossy leaves of *Bergenia* and the needle-like leaves of *Gypsophila*, all doing the same job but looking very different from each other.

So, if leaves are there just to gather light, how come there is such a range of shapes, sizes and colours? Why aren't they just as big and as green as possible? The reason is that they have to do their light gathering under a variety of conditions and they have to stay alive while they're doing it.

In the millions of years that it has taken plants to spread around the world, they have evolved to fit into a wide range of habitats. Plants can be found in the hottest, coldest, wettest and driest parts of the world. In adapting to these different conditions they have developed distinct leaf shapes and textures to help them get the most out of their habitat. Developing an understanding of why plants are the way they are helps the gardener place them appropriately in the garden.

All plants depend on water to stay alive, and in regions where water is scarce plants have developed various strategies for coping with drought and heat. Leaf adaptations are the most obvious and easy to spot of these strategies.

Right Rosemary relishes blazing sunshine and parched conditions. This is due to hundreds of thousands of years of gradual adaptation that have reduced its leaf surface area and toughened the skin to reduce water loss and protect internal cells.

Far right Lavender is another plant that conjures images of baking heat and evocative scents. Narrow leaves, a coating of hairs and that unmistakable scent all help the plant cope with extremes of heat and dryness.

Take a look at all the plants you use to give a Mediterranean feel to your garden: lavender, rosemary, *Yucca*, *Cistus*, *Phlomis*, sage, *Helianthemum*, thyme and, if your climate is mild enough, *Agave* and *Cordyline*. They all have leaves that are able to withstand heat and reduce water loss. It is no coincidence that many of them are silvery grey, thick and tough, as well as aromatic or hairy.

KEEPING THEIR COOL

If you first try to understand how water is lost from a leaf and how a plant controls or reduces that loss, it will help develop a feeling for the characteristics of different types of plant and where best to use them in the garden.

On the undersurface of a leaf there are many tiny pores called stomata (see also page 13). On each square centimetre of an apple leaf – roughly the size of your forefinger nail – there are likely to be 39,000 stomata. Each stoma lets out water vapour. A mature maple in midsummer can lose up to 200 litres (44 gallons) an hour through these pores, effecting the same evaporating cooling process that spilled petrol or nail varnish remover has on your skin.

In a plant's lifetime as much as 98 per cent of the water taken up by the roots is lost as water vapour from the leaves, helping to keep it cool. Take a bare-footed step off a hot patio on to the lawn and notice the difference in temperature, though each is receiving the same amount of heat from the sun. The difference is that each blade of grass is dissipating heat by evaporation and keeping itself below what might otherwise be a lethal temperature. Plants have to balance this water loss and its cooling effect against the amount of water available and the need to maintain a certain level of moisture within its tissues. If water is in short supply, the plant needs some way of reducing any loss from the leaves.

A spherical shape has the smallest surface area for a given volume, and for a plant trying to reduce water loss from its exposed surface, like this cactus, it is the most effective shape. A protective coating of hairs and spines will also help.

So, why don't plants in hot climates just do away with stomata altogether to save water? Well, some cacti have moved as near to that position as possible. Their leaves are no more than spines, and they have reduced the number of stomata to a bare minimum and buried them deep in the pleats of the stem or among a mat of hairs and spines. But while stomata play a vital role in keeping the plant cool, their main purpose is to allow gasses in and out of the plant. Carbon dioxide and oxygen are needed to supply the plant with energy to fuel its internal processes, but you cannot have a hole that lets gasses in and out without water vapour also passing through. In response to this dilemma, many succulents have developed a storage system that allows them to open their stomata fully only at night so that they can take in carbon dioxide when it is cooler, thereby minimizing water loss. They then store carbon dioxide in the leaf and release it internally during daylight hours when their stomata are all but closed.

Alternative solutions

Other plants have adopted different tactics. Some have developed hairs on their leaves, in effect providing their own shade, and if the hairs are silvery, as many of them are, they will reflect a good deal of the sun's heat before it reaches the leaf. A white or silvery skin of a leaf also acts in the same way.

The simple adaptation of having small or narrow leaves, like thyme or the curry plant (*Helichrysum italicum*), reduces the number of stomata and, consequently, water loss. In lavender and rosemary this strategy is even more effective because their leaves roll in on themselves, protecting the stomata. Lavender has taken water conservation one step further by having not only incurved leaves enclosing the stomata but also an undersurface that is covered with tiny hairs to impede water loss even more. As well as providing the leaf with shade, hairiness is a water-saving strategy employed to a greater or lesser extent by many plants. Hairs on the underside of the leaf slow down nearby air movement, so that moisture is carried away less quickly. They also raise the humidity immediately next to the leaf surface, which also reduces evaporation – we all know how difficult it is for sweat to evaporate when the humidity is high. Lavender also produces volatile oils, and it is possible that by increasing the density of the air immediately next to the plant, the oils reduce evaporation. Dittany (*Dictamnus albus*) also produces volatile oils but in such concentration that it has been known to catch fire, hence its alternative name of burning bush.

Plants use fleshy or succulent leaves for storing water and, once stored, the plant needs to make sure it loses as little of it as possible. It can do this by coating the leaf with a waxy or tough skin. Take a leaf from one of the sedums,

It is easy to jump to conclusions about a plant's adaptations. Hairs that might look like a development to help preserve water or protect a plant from the sun may in fact be a defence against cold nights, as with this *Echeveria*. Knowing a plant's native habitat gives a better understanding of why it has certain features.

let's say *Sedum telephium*, and bend it in two like a hinge, then carefully twist the two pieces apart. The thick, quite tough protective layers of cells will peel off like a skin to reveal the glistening, moist and fleshy inside of the leaf.

It is a curious thing that adaptations for coping with heat and drought have given rise to characteristics not very different from those of plants adapted to cold and exposed environments. The low bun-like shape, which reduces the plant's surface area, is common to both. In hot habitats this enables plants to retain water against the heat of the sun and hot drying winds, while in cold habitats it allows plants to retain it in the face of cold desiccating wind. Many succulents have waxy crusted surfaces just as many alpine saxifrages have tough lime-encrusted leaves; both serve to reflect the sun's harsh rays and reduce

water loss. In their natural habitat alpines have to endure a different kind of drought in winter when water is frozen and unavailable to the plants. So adapted are alpines to a dry environment that prolonged wet causes them to rot. For this reason, they need free-draining soil in rockeries and alpine beds, or to be grown in well-vented alpine houses where we control the amount of water they receive.

The succulent and hardy houseleeks (*Sempervivum*) are very similar in appearance to the tender fleshy succulents of arid climates. Although from very different climates, each stores water in its leaves in preparation for dry periods. *Sempervivum arachnoideum* even covers itself with a web of hairs, just like many cacti do.

In different parts of the world native plants have evolved along similar lines and come up with the same types of adaptation to deal with the climatic conditions. If you compare the cactus family of North, Central and South America with the mainly African succulent euphorbias, you will see many similarities between their reduced or non-existent leaves and swollen, pleated stems, despite the fact that they have developed thousands of miles apart on different continents.

MICROCLIMATES

There is some inexplicable part of the gardener's psyche that makes him want to grow what common sense tells him he should not. If you live in an area where the soil has a high pH, you're bound to want to grow acid-loving plants; if your garden has a dry sandy soil, you'll want to grow bog plants, and so on. We are never satisfied, and rather than go with what the land allows, we often choose to go against the flow and make a lot of work for ourselves trying to achieve what nature never intended. I must admit that I have some sympathy for this way of thinking because it means you end up growing a bigger range of plants and, after all, plants are what gardening is all about.

One of the challenges we may set ourselves is to grow plants that in our heart of hearts we know to be tender but we try to convince ourselves that, maybe, we can just get them through the winter outdoors. To do this we make use, either consciously or subconsciously, of what are known as microclimates.

In even the smallest of gardens there are areas that experience different conditions from the rest. A very obvious example is where a south-facing house wall (we are talking northern hemisphere here) gets the full effects of the summer sun and the maximum benefit from the low winter sun. This will create a warmer spot than on the north side of the house, which may receive no sun at all. These different 'climates' within the garden are called microclimates. While the term is often used to describe warmer parts of the garden, it also applies to any area with conditions that differ from those prevailing in the rest of the site, such as a particularly cold section or a corner sheltered from the wind.

By grouping together plants that suit these microclimates we can give each part of the garden a distinct character, as well as knowing that we have given the plants the most suitable growing conditions. Plants with similar requirements make natural-looking companions, even when they come from different parts of the world. Using the shelter and extra warmth that is absorbed by and reflected from a south-facing wall allows you to grow a number of plants that might be less reliably hardy in other parts of the garden. House walls leak a certain amount of heat from within, and during the winter this can help raise the temperature just enough for plants placed close to the wall to escape frost damage. Plants to try in these spots include varieties of *Cistus*, *Melianthus major*, *Amaryllis belladonna*, *Convolvulus cneorum*, *Coronilla valentina* subsp. *glauca*, *Teucrium fruticans* and *Myrtus communis*.

Many half-hardy plants dislike the combination of winter wet and cold. Even in sheltered places it is important to make sure the soil is well drained, although, surprisingly, you may find that in winter the soil at the foot of a wall is dry because of its aspect (the direction in which the wall faces) or the shelter provided by overhanging eaves. As well as casting a rain shadow on the soil, the wall itself absorbs moisture from the ground. In summer the foot of a wall can be particularly dry and newly planted specimens are going to need extra care and watering while they get established. Warm walls can be used to grow plants that are perfectly hardy but that benefit from the extra light and warmth, to prolong the season and ripen their shoots. Fruiting pears are traditionally trained against a south wall to prevent frost damage to their early flowers, as are vines, to ensure ripening of the grapes. *Wisteria* and evergreen *Ceanothus* are two ornamental plants that benefit from a sunny wall.

Localized effects

Anyone who has cycled along a country lane in short sleeves under a clear sky on a cool late summer evening will realize that there can be other localized temperature differences. Warm air gets trapped under the leaf canopy and as you cycle along you will notice very marked differences in temperature under trees. Similarly, in the garden the leaf canopy of evergreens and even the bare branches of deciduous trees and bushes diminish the effects of ground frost. They do this by reducing the amount of heat lost from the soil by radiation on clear nights. This is not a guarantee against prolonged cold weather but it can provide sufficient protection to get plants through cold snaps. I have successfully overwintered dahlia tubers in the dry ground at the foot of an evergreen hedge when there has been no other space – hungry mice were more trouble than the cold.

Another localized condition is the frost pocket. Cold air is heavier than warm air, and on calm cold nights the air sinks to the ground and rolls downhill to accumulate in valley bottoms. In gardens that are on a slope, cold air runs downhill until it meets a barrier such as a hedge or wall or fence. This barrier acts as a dam and the cold air fills up behind it, forming a frost pocket. A fruit garden in a frost pocket is at greater risk of late frost damage to its blossom. In addition, at the other end of the season dahlias, pelargoniums and other tender bedding plants are likely to be taken by the frost much sooner than those that are growing further up the slope.

If your garden is at the bottom of a slope, there is little you can do other than grow late-flowering fruit varieties and tuck your tender plants into spots up against the wall of the building that receives the most sunshine.

In a sloping garden you can take some precautions to avoid frost pockets. Don't have hedges or walls that run across the slope, but if that's impractical, make sure they have openings to let the cold air run through – an open gateway can be enough. Growing plants at risk from frost on the downhill side of a wall or fence helps to protect them from the flow of cold air. Hedges on short clear stems prevent the build-up of cold air by allowing it to flow away under the hedge.

Pot-grown evergreens like *Photinia* x *fraseri* 'Red Robin', box, bay and holly are at risk from drought in the winter on two fronts. First, they may be tucked against a wall where they never get rained on, and who ever thinks of watering their pots in winter? Second, they are at risk if there are long spells of frost. The soil around the roots of plants in containers can freeze solid so that the plant is unable to take up water. However, because these plants are evergreen their leaves are still working, albeit at a reduced rate, and using and losing water. With no water available to replace that used by the leaves, the plant may well die of dehydration if the soil stays frozen for long enough.

Harsh conditions have encouraged some plants like *Pinus montezumae* to retain their leaves to save the precious energy needed to replace them every year. Older leaves low down the stem are gradually shed as their work is done more efficiently by newer leaves.

LEAF LOSS

Why are some trees and plants deciduous and others evergreen? Strictly from a gardener's point of view, it is difficult to understand why one plant loses its leaves and its neighbour does not. What confuses the picture even more is that most plants in the garden are not growing in their natural environment, so there are no clues about their behaviour that might have been gleaned from taking their surroundings into account.

The reason that many plants shed their leaves is that it is a good strategy for surviving the winter. The main danger to plants from freezing temperatures is that ice crystals form in the water in the cells, rupturing the cell walls – we have all seen the resulting mush when we forget to bring tender bedding plants in on a frosty night. Deciduous plants avoid this risk by dropping their leaves in response to the shortening length of the days in autumn. If there are no leaves on a plant, they cannot suffer from frost damage.

Just before the leaves drop, the plant starts to withdraw nutrients from them. A layer of cells then develops between the base of the leaf and the stem. This layer, called an abscission layer, eventually seals off the leaf from the parent plant and the leaf falls to the ground. All this is possible because of a pigment called phytochrome, which is present in many parts of the plant. Phytochrome is able to sense the shortening of the days and so signal to the plant that it is time to start preparing for winter. It can do this long before there is a noticeable change in temperature, and this may explain why herbaceous perennials start to develop overwintering buds well before there is any feel of chill in the air. Phytochrome is also responsible for some seeds needing specifically either dark or light conditions to germinate. It also tells a seedling pushing up from deep below ground that it has reached the light and can start turning green and produce leaves. Phytochrome controls flowering in plants like chrysanthemums, detecting the length of the day or night and triggering the initiation of flower buds only when a specific day length arrives. Commercial chrysanthemum growers overcome this restriction on flower production by artificially providing blackout or lighting to manipulate flowering times.

If losing its leaves is a plant's strategy for surviving the winter, this prompts the question why are plants from some of the coldest regions evergreen? The answer is that plants have developed different ways of coping with low temperatures. In cold areas overall plant activity and the rate of growth can be slow because of the low temperature, frozen ground and a relatively short growing season. The plant does not have the time to grow a new set of leaves each year, so it hangs on to them. It's also possible that nutrient levels may be low and the energy needed to grow a new set of leaves each year is a luxury that cannot be afforded. These factors affect lofty conifers and tiny alpine plants alike.

There are certain evergreen plants, such as privet, that ordinarily keep their leaves throughout the winter but drop them if the weather turns exceptionally cold. This action is reflected by plants that shed leaves in extreme heat to prevent themselves from becoming desiccated.

Even if it loses its leaves, a plant still needs an alternative strategy to protect itself from extreme cold and stop the sap in its trunk and branches from freezing. Plants that have to survive cold winters go through a process of hardening as cold weather approaches. They move water out of the cells and into the spaces between the cells where, if the water freezes, it does less damage. However, since this process can put the cells at risk of death from dehydration, some plants produce a protein that guards against drying out. Plants also produce a natural antifreeze in the stems, and by increasing the levels of sugars in the sap, they can lower its freezing point.

Leaves of conifers from high altitude and extremely cold areas are remarkably resistant to frost. Species of pine and Douglas firs can withstand temperatures down to -40°C (-40°F) without ice crystals being formed in the leaves. Many conifers have developed an ability to be able to carry out photosynthesis (see page 12) at very low temperatures and the angle and arrangement of their branches means that they are well suited to gathering the low-angled light found at extreme northern and southern latitudes.

Most perennial plants have a store of energy either in thick roots or fat dormant buds to see them through the winter and to provide for the rapid growth needed in spring. Even bare-branched, dormant-looking trees will have energy stored in their roots, which they will use to make new roots through the winter despite their inactive appearance. You can take advantage of this unseen winter activity by planting trees and shrubs in the autumn so that, come the spring, they have already started to establish themselves.

Deciduous trees shed their leaves to sit out the winter in a semi-dormant state. With the massive structure of these horse chestnut trees exposed, it is awe-inspiring to think that, apart from a crucial but small volume of chemicals, this great bulk of timber has been built from elements as tenuous as a gas, water and sunlight.

Plumbing

the depths

Getting down to the roots

Roots seem to come up as a topic of conversation only when they are deemed a nuisance, such as when they block your drains, break up the paving on your drive or, worse still, damage the footings of your house. But roots deserve a little more consideration and respect, and most definitely should not be underestimated.

Roots have two important functions – to provide the plant with water and food, and anchor it in the ground – and plants have developed two main types of root to perform them: the taproot and the fibrous root.

TAPROOTS

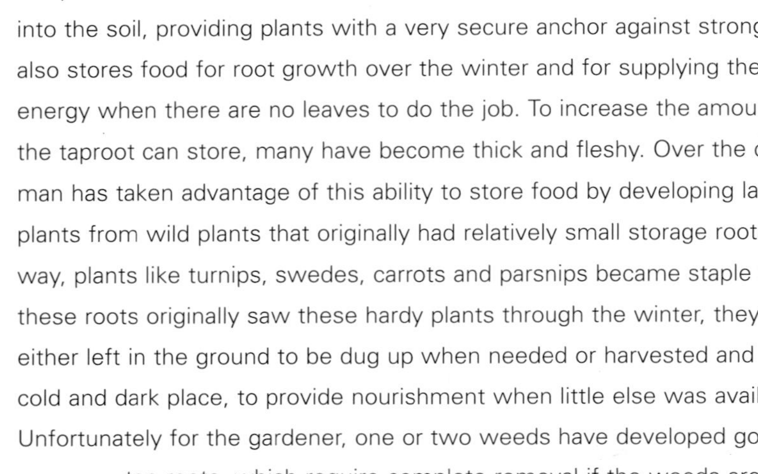

A taproot is a thick root that branches very little and grows straight down, deep into the soil, providing plants with a very secure anchor against strong winds. It also stores food for root growth over the winter and for supplying the plant with energy when there are no leaves to do the job. To increase the amount of food the taproot can store, many have become thick and fleshy. Over the centuries, man has taken advantage of this ability to store food by developing large-rooted plants from wild plants that originally had relatively small storage roots. In this way, plants like turnips, swedes, carrots and parsnips became staple foods. Since these roots originally saw these hardy plants through the winter, they could be either left in the ground to be dug up when needed or harvested and stored in a cold and dark place, to provide nourishment when little else was available. Unfortunately for the gardener, one or two weeds have developed good strong tap roots, which require complete removal if the weeds are not to regrow. Docks are one such species. If you have tried pulling out a dandelion, you will realize how deep and secure its tap root is, and how the stored energy is able to generate new shoots, even from many centimetres down, if you do not manage to get out all the root.

FIBROUS ROOTS

With a fibrous root system, there is no one main root but many lesser roots. Compared to the taproot they do not go deep into the earth, but instead ramify through an unbelievable amount of soil. A single cabbage plant is likely to spread its roots through five cubic metres (175 cubic feet) of soil. This shows the importance of good ground preparation and the maintenance of deep, crumbly soils in the vegetable garden to allow maximum root development.

Dense mats of fibrous roots are good for holding the soil together on steep banks and to bind sandy soils. Plants that spread across the surface and put down fibrous roots as they go are ideal for this purpose; they include plants like many of the ivies, *Symphytum grandiflorum, Geranium macrorrhizum* and *Vinca minor.*

Some trees, such as beech, have surprisingly shallow roots, as can be seen when they are blown out of the ground in a storm. Rather than having deep tap roots, these trees rely on a large spread of roots near the surface to give them support, much as the foot of a wine glass makes the glass stable, although the roots will spread well beyond the leaf canopy.

Fibrous roots are able to respond to the presence of nutrients and water and will grow towards areas where they are available. For me this is a good argument for never planting a hedge where a fence or wall could be used instead and particularly when the hedge runs along a border. The more you nourish and improve the soil in your border, the more the roots of the hedge will enjoy it, invading the soil and taking up valuable food and water that is needed by the other plants growing there. This is also the case if you try to grow border plants under or near to trees, which results in a continual battle to supply sufficient water and nutrients to those plants.

Fibrous roots never stop in their search for water, which means that they will search out the cracks in drains, pushing themselves in and eventually blocking the drain with the amount of root growth formed inside the pipe.

Since roots respond to water, it is important when watering during dry spells to either give a good soaking or none at all. Regular light watering will encourage roots to the surface where they are prone to drying out when the soil does. An occasional good drenching will keep them down in the soil where there is likely to be a more regular supply of moisture. Bear in mind that much of the rain falling on a tree or large shrub is deflected away from the trunk by the leaves and tends to run off in a line under the circumference of the branch tips. It is here and beyond that the roots are most active. Watering the base of the trunk of an established plant will not have any great effect. Equally, it must be remembered that before the roots of a newly planted shrub get out into the surrounding soil, the plant will be relying on the moisture in the original compost around the roots, and this may well dry out despite the fact that the surrounding soil is moist. Give

Above Parsnips have been bred to produce very swollen tap roots, which store and provide as much food as possible.

Far left On steep slopes where the ground needs to be stabilized, the small evergreen periwinkle *Vinca minor* forms a useful binding mat of fibrous roots holding the soil in place.

the pot a good soaking before planting and check regularly until the plant is established. Another factor when establishing plants is the importance of keeping grass away from the base of newly planted trees and shrubs. If allowed to grow right up to the plant, grass roots are in direct competition for water, air and nutrients. Keep an area about a metre in diameter free from grass and weeds around each plant. This will greatly improve the plant's growth rate, and any water or fertilizers applied will benefit the plant, not the grass. It also reduces the risk of damaging the bark with strimmers or lawnmowers.

Water on the move

The task of supplying the plant with water and dissolved nutrients is a considerable one – a mature maple on a breezy summer day can use over 200 litres (44 gallons) an hour. See how long it takes to put just 50 litres (11 gallons) of petrol in your car, and you get some idea of the quantity of water moving into the roots and up the trunk. It should come as no surprise how difficult it is to establish plants around trees when this amount of water is being withdrawn. To be able to meet this demand, roots must penetrate every centimetre of soil within the root zone with an extensive network of ever-finer roots in their efforts to draw in sufficient nutrients and water.

Roots may have to extend to considerable depths or spread to surprising distances to satisfy the plant's needs. The humble wheat plant goes down 1.5m (5ft), while some desert plants can put roots down to 30–40m (100–130ft) in search of deep underground sources. Although you might expect cacti to have deep questing roots, many have a mass of fibrous roots spreading out just below the surface. These are shrivelled and dormant when the weather is at its hottest and driest, but as soon as it rains they swell up and are very quickly able to take in water for storage in the fleshy stems or leaves.

When you dig up an established plant, you invariably cut off many of the roots, and so you do not get any real idea of how extensive or complex the root system might be. However, the following example might very well surprise you and give you some new-found respect for the lowly root. Scientific studies have shown that a mature rye plant, which is only a grass after all, produces an extra five kilometres (three miles) of root each day when grown under ideal conditions. This is, of course, not a single root going out in a straight line but the addition of all the tiny amounts of each individual root's daily extension. If you take into account the amount of root hairs (see below) produced, the total length of effective root added each day is estimated at between 80 and 90 kilometres (50 and 55 miles)! The total root length of the mature plant was estimated at more than 600 kilometres (370 miles) plus over 10,000 kilometres (6,200 miles) of root hairs. Let me emphasize that these staggering figures apply to a humble annual cereal grass and not to some vast tree.

Left The variegated *Euonymus fortunei* is a naturally spreading bush with branches that root as they spread, but if given a wall, it will climb, attaching itself to the wall as it goes. This habit makes it one of the most useful plants for lightening a shaded wall.

Far left *Cornus alba* and its varieties readily produce roots from their stems – you can see this happen for yourself if you place twigs in a jar of water. If pieces of stem as long and as thick as a pencil are pushed into the ground in early winter, they will use stored energy to produce roots and then put out leaves in the spring. The ease with which the stems root makes it easy for the gardener to propagate new plants.

walls or climb into trees. (It is a myth that ivy penetrates the tree it grows on and draws nourishment from it; the stem roots are for climbing only. See page 74.)

A number of plants, including *Actinidia, Amelanchier, Cornus, Elaeagnus, Ligustrum, Rhododendron, Viburnum* and *Wisteria* produce roots on their stems when they bend and touch the ground. In nature many of them use this as a means of spreading, but is also a useful way for gardeners to propagate those plants. Peg the branches tight to the ground and cover them with some gritty compost. Roots will form and, eventually, the rooted section can be removed and potted up as a new plant.

One of the main nutrients used by plants is nitrogen (see page 12). In soils where it is in short supply, certain plants, mostly members of the pea family – legumes – but also the common alder *Alnus glutinosa* and the bog myrtle *Myrica gale*, have developed a technique for obtaining extra supplies. They produce nodules on their roots that are inhabited by bacteria. In return for a supply of sugars, the bacteria take nitrogen from the atmosphere (remember that there are a lot of air spaces in a healthy soil) and make it available to the plant. These nodules are easily seen on the roots of beans, peas, lupins, brooms, *Baptisia* and a host of other plants, including clover. This explains why, when the rest of your lawn is looking pretty tired, the clover, which in effect has its own nitrogen supply, will still look as green as ever.

All things bright

and beautiful

Sense appeal

It would be nice to think that all the wonderful colours and scents we experience in the garden are there just for our enjoyment. But each plant has a far more selfish reason for putting on a colourful display and filling the air with scent, which in some cases can be more accurately described as foetid than delicious.

Oh to be a bee to get views like this. Plants make things as easy as possible for visiting insects by displaying bold 'nectar this way' signs in dots, stripes and ultraviolet markings that bees and insects can interpret.

No plant can afford to waste energy just looking pretty and smelling nice for us. There is no survival value in that; in fact the opposite might be true – the more attractive and sweetly scented the flower, the more likely we are to pick it and use it to make up a bouquet. Each splash of colour is designed to attract insects or birds and guide them to the nectar within the flower, which will, in turn, bring about the pollination of the flower.

COLOUR

Insects see a different range of colours from mammals and birds, including the ultraviolet range of light that is invisible to us. Flowers are not always just a single colour; they often have stripes or dots as well – think of the elaborate pattern of dots on a foxglove flower or the spots and stripes on some *Salvia* and *Alstroemeria*. Although these add to our appreciation of the flowers, they are really intended to direct the pollinator, whether insect or bird, to the nectar it is after and therefore the pollinating parts of the flowers. There are also a great number of flowers without obvious markings to us, but many have guide strips that reflect ultraviolet light and are visible only to insects and birds.

There is a remarkable range of flower colours available to the gardener, and it is this vast choice, with all its variety and subtlety, that makes designing with colour in the garden such an emotional and exciting experience, no matter on what scale you try it or how transient it is. You are working with a palette not only of colour but also of texture, shape and season. Blending all these together and producing a successful mix of plants with harmonizing or contrasting colours is immensely satisfying, though not always as easy as it sounds.

Pigments

Virtually all of the plant colours that we see come from two groups of pigments: carotenoids and anthocyanins. As you might expect from the word association with carrots, carotenoids provide orange coloration, but they are responsible for yellow and some reds, too. Anthocyanin comes from the Greek for 'blue flower', so-called because the first pigments were extracted from a blue flower, but we now know that they are responsible for a far wider range of colours including crimson and purple.

Within a single flower there is often a range of subtle tones and colours. The depth of a colour is determined by the concentration of a given pigment. It could go from a pale coloured, sparse concentration at the petal edge to a

coating on the stems of *Rubus cockburnianus* and *R. biflorus* are all strong elements for a season when there is little else in the garden to inspire.

Let us not forget that green is a colour and the wide range of shades it offers make it invaluable. While green chlorophyll performs a vital function in generating a plant's energy, it is also an extremely important design tool for the gardener. Green used as a foil for brighter colours gives them added intensity and when used alone it has a strong calming and cooling effect in the garden.

Variegation

Variegated plants provide the gardener with another design element, although it can be difficult placing them successfully in the garden. But why are plants variegated in the first place, and why do variegated plants sometimes lose their variegation and become green again?

In some plants what might look like a type of variegation caused by unusual growth is, in fact, the natural way for the plant to grow. The veining or marbling of the leaves of *Arum italicum* subsp. *italicum* 'Marmoratum' and the biennial Our Lady's milk thistle (*Silybum marianum*) are examples of this. The patterning in both plants is caused by air cavities under the skin of the leaf.

CHIMERAS

These are responsible for the most common type of variegation, which arises where the growing tip of a plant has not behaved normally and has produced layers of cells without green pigment. (Chimera very loosely means two genetically different types of cell growing in layers, one within the other; in Greek mythology, a chimera is a fire-breathing monster with a lion's head, goat's body and serpent's tail.) At the very tip of a stem or new leaf there is an area of rapidly dividing cells where all the new growth is made. These cells form in layers. If you imagine putting three translucent white gloves on one hand, one on top of the other, and think of each finger as a shoot tip and each glove as a layer of cells originating at the shoot tip, you'll get a very simple idea of what's going on. The way these cells subsequently develop can lead to several different sorts of variegation in a leaf.

Let's look at two simple examples. Imagine a finger as the green centre of the tiny leaf bud and that you are wearing two translucent white gloves, which represent two layers of cells with no pigment. Imagine your fingertip as this tiny leaf bud and that as it grows and expands it becomes broader and flattens to produce the leaf blade. The white layers would then be stretched thinly across the leaf blade, allowing the green to show through. However, at the edges of the leaf the white would be thicker and no green would be seen. This gives the effect of a white edge to the leaf. Imagine now that your fingertip is white because it has a layer of cells with no pigment and you put on two translucent green gloves. As the leaf develops and flattens out, the green would stretch thinly, allowing

Plants do things for a reason, so there has to be an advantage to the development of bands of white and pink pigmentation on the leaves of the ornamental climber *Actinidia kolomikta*. It certainly looks attractive and it may create the initial interest to bring insects near enough to the plant to discover the small scented flowers.

the unpigmented underlayer to show and the green would be thickest at the edge. The leaf would then appear as green-edged with a white centre.

Occasionally all the cells in a plant become white, and the shoots and leaves produced have no colour; this seems to happen quite often with variegated holly. The temptation is then to try and root all the white shoots as cuttings. Unfortunately, a plant that does not produce chlorophyll cannot produce its own energy and so cannot survive.

Just as a growing tip can mutate to produce layers of cells with no pigment, so the reverse can happen, with unpigmented cells becoming green and resulting in only green leaves being produced. The danger here is that as the completely green leaves and shoots produce more energy than their green and white counterparts, they grow more vigorously and can soon overwhelm the variegated parts of the plant until they are lost completely. Totally green leaves and shoots on a variegated plant must be cut out as soon as they are noticed, otherwise your prized specimen plant will end up an ordinary green one. The same thing happens when either a variegated plant or a weak-growing variety is grafted on to a plain strong rootstock that sends out its own shoots. The shoots of the rootstock soon outgrow the ornamental graft if they're not regularly pruned out.

GENES

The variegated plant that I find the most dramatic of all is a very bold and bright version of the common or garden horseradish (*Armoracia rusticana* 'Variegata').

The 'variegation' in this ornamental biennial *Silybum marianum* is caused by air blisters within the leaf – this is the normal state of the plant and not a disease or mutation. However, there are diseases that cause similar effects. Silver leaf, a disease of plums, is caused by a fungus that causes the tissue in the leaf to separate and allow air in, giving it a silvery appearance.

Its huge leaves are splashed and dashed with creamy white and, provided it is well grown, it provides an exciting focus in the garden, alhough its vigorous spreading habit means it is best contained in a pot. The variegated plant that I like least of all is the rather sick-looking, bun-shaped nasturtium *Tropaeolum* 'Alaska'. Malfunctioning genetic switches are the reason for the variegation in both of these plants. Put simply, this means that the genes controlling the production of pigment get turned on and off in a random manner, causing unpredictable patterns of variegation on the leaves.

VIRAL MARKINGS

Plants with variegation caused by viruses are far fewer than was once thought, but there are some that have established themselves as useful ornamental plants. The climbing Japanese honeysuckle *Lonicera japonica* 'Aureoreticulata' (*aureo* meaning golden, *reticulata* netted) has, as its name suggests, a pattern of bright yellow veining over its leaves caused by a viral infection. *Abutilon pictum* 'Thompsonii', a tender plant often used in the conservatory or on the summer patio, is infected with a mosaic virus that causes an attractive mottled yellow and green variegation on the leaves (see also page 96). The virus seems to do little harm to the plant; it certainly doesn't look sickly and with good growing conditions it looks very fresh and vibrant. The sprawling *Abutilon megapotamicum* 'Variegatum' is another virus-infected plant; mottled leaves enhance the effect of its yellow and red flowers considerably.

Due to genetic mutation, plants occasionally put out shoots that are different from the rest; they might have larger or different coloured flowers or leaves. These are called 'sports' and by propagating from them, new varieties can be established. This holly has sported an all-white shoot but without chlorophyll it, unfortunately, has no chance of growing if removed from the parent plant.

The bog plant *Lysichiton camtschatcensis* produces huge white sweet-smelling spathes to attract pollinating insects in early spring. The flowers are followed by equally impressive large paddle-like leaves that give off a musky odour when crushed, earning it the common name of skunk cabbage.

FRAGRANCE

Scents are complex compounds – ask any perfumier – and flower scents can be composed of up to 150 different types of scent molecule. Plants use scent to attract insects to their flowers, so it's not surprising that scent can be produced by petals, sepals, pollen and even nectar. What might be more surprising is that within each flower there can be different concentrations of scent aimed specifically at guiding the insect to the nectar.

We usually think of bees as the main pollinators. They are especially attracted to sweet, honey-like scents from such flowers as broom (*Spartium junceum*) and tree lupin (*Lupinus arboreus*). But in many areas, particularly cooler parts of the world, flies carry out most of the pollinating. Like bees, flies are drawn to sweet-smelling flowers but they also like mustier and, to us, less appealing scents like those of rowan (*Sorbus aucuparia*) and hawthorn (*Crataegus monogyna*).

Humans have a very poor sense of smell compared to that of a bee. Bees are able to detect scents between ten and one hundred times weaker than those discernible by us. Imagine the sea of scents they must fly through. Much as we can cut out extraneous noise and focus on what we want to hear, so the bee can ignore the meaningless scents to select and home in on the one it wants.

Flies can detect the perfume of a flower at least two metres (six feet) away and, even though they may not be able to see the flower, they are able to track it down via its scent. Some flowers like *Arum maculatum* and those of the succulent *Stapelia* produce scents that are far from sweet smelling. *Stapelia* emit a foetid odour like rotting meat to attract flies, while the *Arum* gives off a smell resembling dung to attract its small pollinating insects.

There are, of course, plenty of delicious smells in the garden. Inhale the scent of *Cosmos atrosanguineus* flowers. Do you detect more than a hint of cocoa? What about the flowers of *Iris gramineus*? Do they make you think of plum tart? Give the leaves of *Melianthus major* a rub and see if you smell peanut butter.

Energy efficient

As with all plant functions, there is little wasted energy when it comes to scent production; it is only switched on when it is likely to be most effective. Scent production is reduced on cold dull days when there are likely to be fewer insects flying. Even when conditions are good, it may take on a daily rhythmic cycle, according to the targeted insect. If the plant needs to attract moths, then scent is needed in the evening and is not to be wasted during daylight hours. If you take a sniff of *Nicotiana sylvestris, Matthiola bicornis* and *Oenothera biennis* in the daytime, you will be less than impressed with their scent, but come the evening they pour their fragrance into the garden. Many flowers that produce scent in the daytime have their peak production in the early afternoon, which coincides with the warmest time of the day when insects are at their most active.

Above On a warm day bend down and take a sniff of the dark flowers of *Cosmos atrosanguineus*. You will smell the unmistakable aroma of cocoa, which has led to it being called the chocolate cosmos.

Left Plant scents can whisk you off on a culinary world tour. *Helichrysum italicum* subsp. *serotinum*, pictured here, has an authentic curry smell.

Below As evening comes you will be struck by the strong fragrance of *Nicotiana*. The scent is produced to coincide with the activity of their main pollinators, night-flying moths.

Getting a grip

Climbing the walls

Have you ever wondered what roses, vines and wisteria climbed up before gardeners provided walls, trellising and wires?

Obviously, nature provided the support, and it is by understanding how plants got a grip on what nature had to offer that we can give our garden plants the support they need. In that way, you can avoid those great birds' nests of honeysuckle and clematis that hang off the front of the house, flopping about in the wind.

Before looking at the different types of climbers, it's important to distinguish between climbing plants and wall shrubs.

There are a number of shrubs that are so often grown against a wall, either for convenience or for the extra protection provided by the wall, that they have become confused with true climbers; the impression given is that they need to have a wall or fence to grow up. Such plants include *Pyracantha, Ceanothus* and *Garrya*, all of which can be grown as freestanding shrubs. They will never naturally cling to a wall or wires and are always going to need tying to their supporting structures if they are not to fall or be at risk from being blown off. Once they find their support, whether wires, wall or another shrub, true climbers will grasp on to it quite naturally and without interference.

In nature, a climber's aim is to be higher up than other plants and as near to the light as possible – this is particularly important if you start life on the woodland floor. Their flowers will then be in the best possible position for being pollinated and dispersing their seed. To help them do this they have developed a number of techniques.

TWINERS

The most obvious way for a plant to climb is with twining stems. Take a look at a honeysuckle or wisteria and you will see that the leading shoots have twisted themselves around whatever is available. If there is nothing else available, they will even twist around themselves. At worst, they may have twined tightly around a drainpipe and be either crushing it or gradually pulling it off the wall with the weight of the plant. My advice is never tuck the shoots behind the pipe, thinking that you will come back later and do a proper job. You probably never will, and the results can be costly.

Twining climbers include some of the most vigorous garden plants like the Russian vine (*Fallopia baldschuanica*) and the ornamental hop (*Humulus lupulus* 'Aureus'), which has the added advantage of rough, downward-facing hairs on the hop stem that help it to grip its host. Then there are the lesser plants like the runner bean, black-eyed Susan (*Thunbergia alata*) and the blue-flowered *Tweedia caerulea*, also known as *Oxypetalum caeruleum*. Anyone who has had

Climbing plants are the wallpaper of the garden. Understanding how they attach themselves to their support will mean that you will not be forever trying to stick the wallpaper back up. Plants such as this Boston ivy (*Parthenocissus tricuspidata*) make life easier because they are self-clinging and require no extra support.

Above Tendrils have a fragile beauty that hides a surprising strength. Once they have secured themselves around a stem and matured, they have a resilience and tenacity that holds them fast against buffeting winds and takes the weight of fruits like melons and gourds.

Far right *Mutisia* has a 'belt and braces' approach to climbing. Not only does it have tendrils at its leaf tips but the long flower stalks also twine around their support.

their plants covered in bindweed (*Convolvulus*) will know that weeds also take advantage of this method of climbing, smothering host plants.

In nature these climbers use the vertical stems of other plants to pull themselves up, so in the garden we should offer them similar conditions. This can be by growing them through other plants or, if we want to train them up a wall or fence, by providing supports like canes or wires that are attached vertically. Garden canes can be very smooth and slippery making it difficult for some twining plants to get started; rougher pieces of stem, perhaps a hazel rod, overcome this problem.

The leading tip of twining plants grows in wide circles until it touches its support, which it then has to be able to wrap around. For this reason, trellising that is set tightly against the wall is not always the best type of support. In addition, some heavy-duty twining plants like wisteria or honeysuckle eventually grow stems so thick that they wrench trellising apart if they are allowed to thread themselves through it when young.

TENDRILS

Many climbers use tendrils, which are derived from different parts of the plant, to attach themselves to their supports. They come in all shapes and sizes, and are sensitive to touch. They reach out until contact is made with something rigid, then the side of the tendril furthest away from the contact grows faster than the side nearest, causing it to wrap around the support.

Having secured their 'fingers' to a twig, wire or trellising, many tendrils perform a neat trick along the stem of the tendril; this can often be seen on the tendrils of the grapevine (*Vitis vinifera*). One end coils clockwise, the other in an anticlockwise direction, creating a spring-like twist at either end of the tendril with

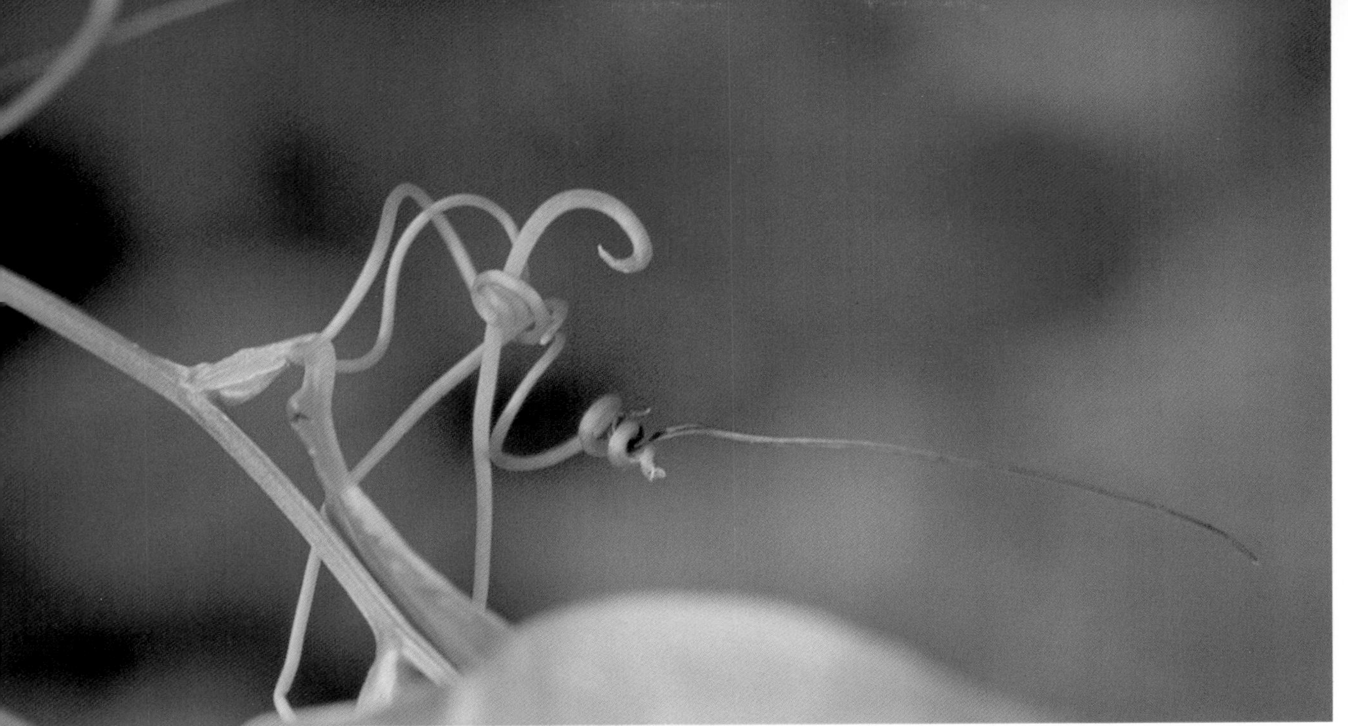

the change of direction in the middle. As it keeps twisting, the vine is drawn closer to its support. Sounds complicated? If you consider it, there can be no other way for it to coil; once both ends are fixed how else can it move?

If you study pea plants or sweat peas, it is easy to see that their tendrils have developed from leaves, with some of them still being part leaf, part tendril. In *Pyrostegia venusta* you can see that the tendril has developed from one of the three stalked leaflets making up the leaf.

Mutisia and *Littonia* have grown thin, grasping ends to their leaves. In the former, these ends have become long thread-like tendrils, which are assisted in their role by the flower stalk itself twining around supporting twigs and branches. There are no obvious signs of tendrils on the common *Clematis montana*, but a close inspection will reveal that the plant uses its leaf stalks as tendrils to wrap around its supporting host. Two showy relatives of the nasturtium employ a similar tactic: *Tropaeolum speciosum* and *T. tuberosum* both clasp their support with their leaf stalks.

Cobaea scandens has tiny hooks at the end of each tendril that it uses as grappling hooks. Having caught a stem, the tendril wraps around and then coils itself to secure the plant.

Since nature has designed tendrils to grip thin branches and twigs, the closer we can emulate that situation, the more secure and natural our climbers will look. Many climbers look their best growing through another plant, but take care to match the vigour of the climber to that of its host. Trellising and wire or nylon netting provide plenty of closely spaced places for plants to grip; small plants need only small twigs or wigwams made from twigs.

One plant with tendrils that can manage without any twiggy supprt is the Boston ivy (*Parthenocissus tricuspidata*). This puts out small hand-like tendrils that, on contact with a rigid surface, produce discs like suckers at the end of each 'finger'. The discs glue themselves to the surface and the tendril coils itself up to pull the stem close to the surface.

STICKY ROOTS

If you have ever been faced with the task of removing ivy from your walls and almost ripped off your fingernails trying to prise it free, you will know how effective are the natural glue and hardened roots that hold the plant fast. Ivy, like the climbing hydrangea (*Hydrangea anomala* subsp. *petiolaris*), sends out shoots that produce roots along the surface that's in contact with the supporting structure. The short roots penetrate any cracks and imperfections where they set, become hardened and hold the stem to its support, whether a wall, fence or tree trunk, with incredible tenacity.

THORNS

Thorns on stems are an adaptation that can benefit a plant in two ways. The obvious one is that they guard against herbivorous animals that might otherwise see the plant, or at least its young shoots or seeds, as a meal. They also help climbing or scrambling plants get their rather thin stems closer to the light

The tendrils of *Parthenocissus* cling to the wall with wiry flat-tipped sticky fingers. Such is their grip that pulling the stems off the wall often leaves the tendril tips still firmly attached. For these fingers to get a hold initially, young plants need to be held firmly against the wall so that they don't blow about.

coming through the tree tops. As a stem grows upwards, it reaches a point where it cannot hold itself upright, and so leans on its nearest neighbour, where its thorns lodge against branches and twigs. This prevents the stem from slipping back to the ground while the top of the shoot forges on again until it eventually gains sufficient height.

Plants with thorns in the garden include roses and brambles, and in the conservatory *Bougainvillea*. There has been so much crossbreeding in shrub roses that many of their characteristics bear little relevance to their original habitat. Most climbing roses, however, do sport great spines, and the nearer they are to the original species, the better examples they are. Let's use the climbing *Rosa filipes* 'Kiftsgate' as an example of a successful climber. A prolific flowerer and ridiculously vigorous (it grows several metres a year), this plant is not far removed from the wild and is a great, although extreme, example of an aggressive climber. Its thrusting stems bear stout thorns that hold it 10–15m (30–50ft) or more up in a tree, where it will either bear down on or smother its host. Fantastic, if you have the space, but it's not for the small garden or the faint-hearted, and not many of us are willing or able to sacrifice a tree, even two or three, so that we can give a rose its head.

There are, however, many lesser climbing roses than *Rosa filipes* 'Kiftsgate' that are also vigorous and hard to manage, so what should we do with them? I shall undoubtedly incur the wrath of rose-lovers everywhere by saying this,

This innocent-looking bramble clambers into trees bending down branches and overwhelming smaller trees. If there are no trees around, it uses its thorns to build itself into great impenetrable mounds that provide the ideal protection for burrowing rabbits.

but to me there is no plant that looks more like a fish out of water than a vigorous climbing rose pinned to a wall. Earlier in this chapter (see page 70) I talked about wall shrubs and true climbers and there is no doubt that these roses are true climbers, but if you want to grow them against a wall, you are going to have to treat them as wall shrubs and tie them in regularly. There is no system that allows you to grow them against a wall in anything resembling a natural way. A tree, large frame or pergola is the best solution.

There are two types of climbing rose – rambling and climbing – and both use thorns to achieve their height. Considerable crossbreeding means that their characters are not always distinguishable. Strictly speaking, a rambler produces long shoots from ground level one year, and flowers on these shoots the next. These are cut out after flowering to make way for the next flush of shoots that will flower next year – exactly the same treatment as raspberries or blackberries.

Ordinary climbing roses can be tied in to their wall or fence to form a framework. The sideshoots are shortened each year, and since the older stems become very thick, they can be cut out at their base to encourage replacement shoots that will sprout from the ground with great vigour the following spring.

Brambles use the same thorny technique as roses to get their flowers and fruit up towards the sun, and they are very good at it. I have seen a yew tree so filled with brambles that, such was the show at flowering time, I began to think how much better the yew tree would look if it carried large heads of pink and white flowers, not to mention glossy black berries to follow.

Bougainvillea fits into the thorny climber category on two counts. If you handle the plant, you will be able to testify to its sharp stem spines, but it has another way of helping itself to climb. When it loses its flowers, some of the flower stalks harden and become woody, thorn-like hooks that are an additional method of securing the plant it as it scrambles around.

It is worth noting here that when the wind hits a wall, particularly that of a tall house, it is accelerated along the face of the wall to a far greater speed than it would be in the open. Climbers growing against walls in exposed positions therefore receive more than their fair share of wind, so it is worth checking their ties regularly, particularly as plants get bigger and top heavy. If the wind hits the wall at right angles, you not only get a rush along the wall but also strong gusts blowing plants away from the foot of the wall.

Keeping the

enemy at bay

An overview

There are hundreds of animals in the world, over a million different types of insects and at least a hundred thousand different types of fungi and viruses.

Given these statistics, what chance does the poor plant have at the base of every food chain? Fortunately, plants know a thing or two about surviving: plant material still makes up 99 per cent of the world's biomass (the total weight of the world's animal and plant population).

Those millions of insects and animals do not all eat living plant material and those that do, do not all kill the plants they feed on. A large proportion does not interfere with garden plants and some are even beneficial. Better still, some insects feed on the insects that feed on garden plants, and these are proving to be useful allies in the control of pests without chemicals (see page 100). Nor are all fungi out to destroy plants. Again, some of them are extremely important to plants and form close partnerships that benefit both plant and fungus. But the most important factor is that plants are resilient survivors and able to cope with almost anything nature throws at them – after all, they have been doing it for millions of years.

It would be intriguing to be able to go back in time and look at plants at, say, every half a million years to see how far their defences had developed. We could also see the see-sawing between a plant developing a defence strategy and the insect pest coming up with a way around it, only to prompt the plant to produce a different toxin or another change in its defences. This constant battle of readjustment is still going on, but such is the time scale of these gradual developments that we don't notice it. That insects are able to develop resistance to toxins is without doubt because several species of common garden and greenhouse pests have done just that. Within a relatively short time, the continued use of one type of insecticide has led to resistant strains of insects making that particular chemical useless. In evolutionary terms this has happened in the blink of an eye. Resistance to fungicides and even some herbicides has also developed for the same reason of over-use.

Trees and shrubs are able to withstand attacks from many of the fungi that invade them but once struck by honey fungus there is virtually no chance of recovery. The fungus uses the decaying wood as a source of food to nourish the mycelium as it spreads out to other plants. There is little that can be done, apart from using a physical barrier to prevent its spread.

HOW PLANTS DEFEND THEMSELVES

Unlike animals, plants cannot run away from would-be predators, but it would be a mistake to think that they just sit there waiting to be eaten. They have a trick or two up their sleeves, and quite complicated ones at that.

The spines on *Pyracantha* and hawthorn, and the stinging hairs on nettles are outward signs that plants can defend themselves against larger grazing and browsing animals. But, apart from protective hairs, there are few visible signs of a plant being active in its battle against smaller pests and diseases. Because the defence mechanisms are internal and discrete, it is easy to underestimate how sophisticated they are.

Above left Though occasionally affected by leaf spots, yuccas are generally pest- and disease-free. The tough leathery leaves are difficult for insects or fungi to penetrate.

Above right There are a number of caterpillars whose only food source is the nettle, despite its stinging hairs, but they never do enough damage to destroy the plant completely. Once cut and wilted, the nettles lose their sting and are safe to handle.

An obvious way for a plant to defend itself against being eaten is to make its leaves, stems or fruit unpalatable or toxic, in the hope that one bite will be enough to discourage or even kill the attacking pest or animal. An example is yew (*Taxus baccata*): the foliage and the seeds in the red berries are lethal to even quite large animals, and this is often cited as a reason why yew was traditionally grown in churchyards away from livestock.

The main constituent of plants is cellulose, which is extremely tough and digestible only by ruminant animals such as horses and sheep. And they can do it only with the help of microbes in the stomach. The microbes 'eat' the cellulose and release excess energy to the animal. What a shame man cannot cope with cellulose: it would certainly take mowing the lawn to another dimension!

Lignin, which makes up the woody part of a plant, is tougher still and to all practical ends indigestible. The leaves of fibrous plants like *Phormium tenax* and *Yucca filamentosa* are too tough for most insects and animals to bother with, and so they are left alone in preference for more succulent species. Insects also find it difficult to lay their eggs in thick-skinned plants.

Toxic chemicals

Certain plants have developed toxic chemicals to put paid to insect attackers. However, not all plants that are poisonous to humans are toxic to insects. Some very toxic substances like curare and strychnine are extracted from plants but there is no evidence to suggest that they are present to protect the plant from insect attack. Pyrethrum was one of the first chemicals to be extracted from plants and used as an insecticide. It was extracted from *Tanacetum cinerariifolium*, a close relative of tansy, which itself is used as an insect repellent. Another early contact insecticide, derris, was extracted from the root of a tree. The main toxic chemical in derris is rotenone.

Many of the insecticides once extracted from plants are now artificially synthesized for cheaper production. They are relatively non-toxic to humans, and their short persistence makes them safe to use on edible crops, although it does not always make them the most effective treatment.

In the garden there are some obvious deterrents to invading insects; the bitter and irritating sap of euphorbia, for example, deters insects not only with its toxicity but also with the amount that is exuded. Dandelions, sow thistles and chicory also produce a bitter but less dangerous sap.

Some plants produce sap that has a greater toxic effect when exposed to a certain level of light, and getting it on your skin on a bright sunny day can cause severe blistering. Light-reactive toxic compounds are found in rue (*Ruta graveolens*) and the giant hogweed (*Heracleum mantegazzianum*), the sap of the latter causing painful blistering of the skin. Less dangerous light-sensitive compounds are found in parsnips and celery, as well as parsley and figs. An insect with a stomach full of these light-activated toxins will certainly not want to get caught out in the sun.

When dealing with any plants that are known to cause allergic reactions, make sure that you take great care because a single exposure can sensitize the skin and set up an allergy to other irritants.

The cabbage holds two substances in special cells in the leaf. When it is attacked by a pest, these two chemicals come together and release a bitter compound to deter the attacker. This sounds as if it's exactly what you'd want if you are growing

In the past, rue has been recommended for the herb garden and even as a culinary herb. But the toxins in the plant have the potential to cause severe blistering. Simply touching it in the garden may cause a reaction in someone with sensitive skin.

cabbages, but here comes the rub. The caterpillar of the cabbage white butterfly has developed an immunity to the toxin and, worse still, it incorporates the toxin into its tissue, making it distasteful to predatory birds. So, the unfortunate result is that you not only have a pest that flouts the plant's defences, but you also have a caterpillar that even the birds won't eat.

Subtle defences

Other chemicals, such as plant alkaloids (complex molecules produced by a plant for its defence, including codeine, morphine and nicotine), are thought to protect plants, although their physical effects are less obvious. These include nicotine, once used as an insecticidal fumigant in greenhouses, and strychnine.

High tannin levels in leaves and, in particular, bark act as a protectant. Oak (*Quercus*), hemlock (*Tsuga*) and wattle (*Acacia*) have high tannin levels in their bark (oak bark is the traditional source of tannin for the European leather trade). If you have tried to eat the fruit of a sloe or medlar, or sucked on a teabag, you will have experienced the astringent and drying effect of tannin, an effect likely to make a browsing animal look elsewhere for food. Tannins destroy the lubricating properties in saliva by binding to the protein in the salivary enzyme. Since enzymes are crucial facilitators in biological processes in plants and animals, the ability of tannins to inactivate enzymes makes them a very useful natural insect deterrent. To prevent the tannins from destroying the plant's own enzymes, they are locked up in the plant until its cells are damaged and then they are released. They also act as a fungicide within the plant to prevent decay, and the mature wood inside trees is protected by high levels of tannins. The effects of tannins that have been ingested are even subtler, suppressing appetite and digestion in cattle and other ruminant animals by reducing microbial activity in the stomach.

Poisonous plants

We are becoming increasingly aware of the dangers of poisonous plants, and more and more of them are marked up as such in garden centres. We have known about most of the more dangerous plants for a long time and take care accordingly. These include the seeds of laburnum, the whole plant but especially the seeds and roots of monkshood (*Aconitum*), potatoes that have gone green and the berries of ivy and privet. Then there is the foxglove, which most of us know can affect the heart because its seeds or leaves are used to make the heart stimulant digitalis. It's perfectly safe to touch a foxglove – just don't eat any part of it.

Other familar garden plants that are poisonous include rhododendrons, *Kalmia*, *Philodendron*, sweat peas, buttercups and anemones. But we are probably more concerned about berries and seeds because children will be tempted to eat them. One of the most deadly poisons, ricin, occurs in the seed coat of the castor oil plant (*Ricinus communis*) and is lethal, even in very small quantities.

Have you taken any cyanide recently? Think twice before you answer: the question isn't as odd as it sounds. If you have ever eaten almonds or swallowed an apple pip or two, you most definitely have. Cyanide is a common defence 'ingredient' in plants. It is normally locked up in the plant but released when it is bitten or chewed by an insect. Cyanide is an ingredient of prussic acid (a solution of hydrogen cyanide in water) and it is what gives almonds their distinctive smell. Take a leaf of *Prunus laurocerasus*, the shiny, large-leaved cherry laurel commonly used for hedging by people with little imagination, and crush it vigorously between your thumb and forefinger. Inhale. At first the leaf just smells 'green', but then a distinct odour of almonds develops – this is due to the presence of prussic acid.

Solanine is another poison found in familiar plants. It is present in potatoes, although not in toxic quantities until the potato is exposed to light and turns green. Under light, far higher levels of solanine are produced and eating a green potato can make you seriously ill. From the potato's point of view, this is the perfect defence, deterring any creature trying to eat its winter store of starch that has, unfortunately, ended up on the soil surface. Although the tuber is poisonous only after it has been exposed to light, the rest of the potato plant, which also contains solanine, is toxic. Similarly, the stems and leaves of tomato and aubergine are toxic. Significantly, both belong to the same family, Solanaceae, as the potato.

Above left Some of our prettiest flowers, such as the wood anemone (*Anemone nemorosa*), have toxic properties, but they would need to be eaten in large quantities to put us at risk. The likelihood of anyone eating their way through an entire herbaceous border is slim.

Above right The toxic properties of monkshood (*Aconitum napellus*) have caused florists to be hospitalized after handling them as cut flowers. There is now greater awareness of the poisonous nature of certain plants, and garden centres are labelling plants accordingly.

Rhubarb is another example of humans coming up against deterrents aimed at animals. There is sufficient oxalic acid in rhubarb leaves to be a serious health threat to any animal or human eating them. The stems, however, contain enough of the acid to give a sharp tanginess that begs for a sweetening dose of sugar but not enough to cause any harm – unless you eat too many raw sticks, when the consequences are inconvenient but not life-threatening. Oxalic acid also gives sorrel its sharp taste.

Sometimes the most innocent-looking plants can harbour unknown risks. I have known a florist end up in hospital after experiencing an allergic reaction to larkspurs delivered to her shop. All parts of various species of delphinium are poisonous and likely to cause a reaction – larkspur is one of those species.

Preventing insect attack

The biggest threat to most plants is from insects. Consequently, the majority of toxins produced by plants have evolved in response to preventing insect attack rather than to deal with the more sporadic damage caused by grazing animals, which need far larger doses of a toxin to be deterred.

The production of any defence chemical, in fact the development of any feature in a plant, is costly in terms of energy. During their evolution plants have had to strike a balance between the energy cost of, for example, having large showy flowers, and the benefit gained. They are very miserly with their energy and do not use it unnecessarily. To this end some species concentrate toxins in the most vulnerable parts of the plant, such as young leaves, rather than produce them throughout the whole of the plant. Another strategy is to have toxins in only some of the leaves and space them randomly on the plant. An attacking insect does not know whether the leaf it is about to eat contains toxins or is palatable, which means that it is likely to have to move between leaves, using up energy and slowing up the process of attack. It also makes the insect more vulnerable to predators as it moves from leaf to leaf.

Much as we might get annoyed by insects eating our garden plants, it is hard not to smile at the damage caused to this rose leaf by the leaf cutter bee. The pieces cut out are taken to holes in walls or old trees and used to form thimble-like cells in which the female bee lays her eggs.

There is also evidence to show that this same strategy takes place in tree populations, where some trees will have overall high levels of defence chemicals and others much lower levels. The energy that an insect wastes sorting out which plant is edible and which is not may be enough to make it move to another species altogether to feed.

If you are not yet in awe of the complexity of plant defences and their subtle conservation of energy, read on. None of the ingenious devices described will be obvious to you in the garden. We know about them only through scientific research, but much of this research was triggered by the careful observation of plant and insect behaviour. While none of us is likely to produce a detailed scientific paper on the complex chemicals in plants, we can gain considerable satisfaction from the close observation of insects and the way they work.

Some plants produce toxins only in response to an attack, instead of having them ever present throughout the plant, which wastes energy. This strategy is employed by a wide variety of species. A tomato plant will respond to an attack on one of its leaves by rapidly producing defence compounds in nearby leaves. But how does one leaf know another is being attacked? That is still something of a mystery, although complex chemical signalling is suspected. What is more intriguing and, for want of a better word, mind-boggling, is that this strategy seems to be carried out on a much larger scale in some species of willow. That an insect attack on one tree triggers the build-up of defence chemicals in that tree is understandable, but the fact that neighbouring trees also start to produce those chemicals borders on the incredible.

Further evidence of plant ingenuity is the fact that some species produce compounds that copy insect hormones. When the attacking insect ingests these hormones, it stops reproducing, leading to a reduction in population.

A similar situation occurs with a certain potato aphid that sends out chemical signals when it is being attacked. This signal warns other aphids to stay away. The potato plant has developed hairs that, when attacked by the aphid, release the same warning chemical, thus driving away further attackers. Don't tell me that plants aren't smart.

INSECT PESTS

Insects are very much a part of gardening life. The goodies help to pollinate flowers, break down the compost heap and some even devour the baddies. In turn, the baddies do their utmost to destroy shoots, deform buds, eat roots, scar fruit and disfigure leaves. It is easy to dislike insects.

There are simply too many insect pests for me to talk about all of them here, so, on the basis that they are my 'favourites', I have chosen two or three common types to look at in some detail. (To clarify, an insect is defined as having three pairs of legs. But, for simplicity, I have included mites under the heading of insects, even though they are not insects, have four pairs of legs and are distantly related to spiders.) By having a closer look at insect pests and by ignoring any adverse effect they may have on your garden, you may find that you start to admire them and see them as fascinating and often beautiful creatures, even if that beauty comes only from their complex and elaborate life cycles.

Although it is a natural reaction to want to eliminate any insect pest damaging your plants, try to get an insight into their behaviour first. If you understand how they feed and breed, you will be better equipped to control them. Most insects cause damage by feeding, but some do so by probing plants in their search for ideal sites for egglaying, removing material for nests or by using the plant to make protective structures. Some have the ability to disrupt the growth pattern of the plant so that it forms abnormal leaves, for example.

Aphids

There are some 500 different types of aphid. They are among the most common insect pests found in the garden, the greenhouse and even indoors on house plants. You are probably more familiar than you would like to be with the ubiquitous greenfly and blackfly. (Strictly speaking, none of these is a true fly because the winged adults have two pairs of wings and to be classified as a true fly, they should have only one pair.)

Curiously, some aphids are very particular about their hosts: the honeysuckle aphid, for example, is found only on honeysuckle, while the peach potato aphid and the glasshouse and potato aphid, despite their names, feed on a wide range of ornamental plants, both indoors and out. This selectivity or lack of it may have something to do with certain aphids overcoming the defences of one type of plant but not others, and thereby becoming exclusive to that plant.

Some aphids find their way underground to the roots of plants such as lettuce, roses and primulas. The lettuce root aphid, for example, lives on the stems of the tall Lombardy poplar (*Populus nigra* 'Italica') in winter but uses the roots of lettuce plants as its alternative summer host (see also page 90). Others, like the artichoke tuber aphid, live permanently on the roots of Jerusalem artichokes.

EATING MACHINES

Aphids are poor fliers but they can be carried hundreds of miles by wind and air currents in their search for food. They react to the colour of plants and find greenish-yellow – the usual colour of young tender tissue – the most attractive. Scent is thought to play a role in their hunt for food but only at distances of less than one metre.

Having found a possible food source, aphids will test it with their mouthparts to see if the plant is tender enough and the sap has sufficient food value. They will choose healthy well-fed plants in preference to those in a poor nutritional state.

Aphids feed by sucking sap through tubular mouthparts that pierce the plant tissue. The sugar-rich but protein-poor sap is taken up in large quantities to extract enough protein to satisfy the aphid. Excess sugar is then excreted as honeydew – a surprisingly attractive name for something that is flicked off the aphid's back end! Wherever the honeydew falls, be it on to the conservatory floor or foliage lower down the plant, it leaves a sticky coating. (Soon this coating will be covered by a dark brown sooty mould that feeds on the honeydew.) Even if you cannot see the aphids, the sticky feel of the honeydew is a giveaway. Ants scurrying up and down are also a sign of aphids at work because they, too, find honeydew nutritious.

Aphids will hunt out the best place on a plant to get their supply of sap. That is why you will often see them close to the leaf veins, which are the main conduits of food to the leaf, and at the growing tips where a lot of food is pushed up the plant to supply the fast-growing cells. Here the immature tissue is soft and easily penetrated. The extraction of sap by aphids may cause poor growth in that part of the plant. In an effort to counter this,

Aphids are a fact of gardening life, but before you reach for the spray gun, take a closer look. Check out these greenfly with their twin exhausts, which are believed to be used for releasing defence chemicals, and see how they line themselves up on the best sap-producing sites.

Given these statistics, what chance does the poor plant have at the base of every food chain? Fortunately, plants know a thing or two about surviving: plant material still makes up 99 per cent of the world's biomass (the total weight of the world's animal and plant population).

Those millions of insects and animals do not all eat living plant material and those that do, do not all kill the plants they feed on. A large proportion does not interfere with garden plants and some are even beneficial. Better still, some insects feed on the insects that feed on garden plants, and these are proving to be useful allies in the control of pests without chemicals (see page 100). Nor are all fungi out to destroy plants. Again, some of them are extremely important to plants and form close partnerships that benefit both plant and fungus. But the most important factor is that plants are resilient survivors and able to cope with almost anything nature throws at them – after all, they have been doing it for millions of years.

It would be intriguing to be able to go back in time and look at plants at, say, every half a million years to see how far their defences had developed. We could also see the see-sawing between a plant developing a defence strategy and the insect pest coming up with a way around it, only to prompt the plant to produce a different toxin or another change in its defences. This constant battle of readjustment is still going on, but such is the time scale of these gradual developments that we don't notice it. That insects are able to develop resistance to toxins is without doubt because several species of common garden and greenhouse pests have done just that. Within a relatively short time, the continued use of one type of insecticide has led to resistant strains of insects making that particular chemical useless. In evolutionary terms this has happened in the blink of an eye. Resistance to fungicides and even some herbicides has also developed for the same reason of over-use.

Above right Not only do we find nasturtium leaves a tangy addition to a salad, black bean aphids also enjoy them, clustering in great colonies on the stalks and underside of the leaves. And even if we manage to control the aphids – pinching out the affected parts is a simple way – we are likely to find cabbage caterpillars munching the leaves. Regular inspection and removal is the key.

Below right Beans seem prone to more than their fair share of pests and diseases, from rots and mildews to eelworms and aphids. To top it all, bees have learnt that by making a hole in the side of the flower they can get straight to the nectar without having to push their way through the mouth of the flower. Unfortunately, this means that the flower is not pollinated and the beans are not set.

HOW PLANTS DEFEND THEMSELVES

Unlike animals, plants cannot run away from would-be predators, but it would be a mistake to think that they just sit there waiting to be eaten. They have a trick or two up their sleeves, and quite complicated ones at that.

The spines on *Pyracantha* and hawthorn, and the stinging hairs on nettles are outward signs that plants can defend themselves against larger grazing and browsing animals. But, apart from protective hairs, there are few visible signs of a plant being active in its battle against smaller pests and diseases. Because the defence mechanisms are internal and discrete, it is easy to underestimate how sophisticated they are.

An obvious way for a plant to defend itself against being eaten is to make its leaves, stems or fruit unpalatable or toxic, in the hope that one bite will be enough to discourage or even kill the attacking pest or animal. An example is yew

There is rarely, if ever, any family connection between an aphid's summer and winter hosts. In fact, they are so dissimilar that together they make rather comic reading. Other two-host combinations, which sound like ideas for the experimental chef, include pear and bedstraw (*Galium*), plums and reeds, damsons and hops, gooseberries and lettuce, currants and lettuce, willows and carrots, and plums and water lilies.

Beetles

Beetles are the largest group of insects, and members of this great order include predatory beetles, like ladybirds, which eat insect pests and are good for the garden. There are also beetles that eat dead plant material, helping to break down organic matter, and those that eat dead wood – these include the woodworm, which, unfortunately, does not appreciate the difference between a dead tree branch and a piece of furniture.

Inevitably, there are beetles that are garden pests. These include the large cockchafers, Colorado beetles, flea beetles, wireworms, lily beetles, elm bark beetles, which carry Dutch elm disease into the elm tree, and weevils.

Weevils form quite a large group of insects, which are a pest to both the vegetable and ornamental gardener. Despite the damage they can do, I have to admit that I feel quite kindly towards weevils. It has something to do with their usually solid look and trundling gait, plus their long 'noses', which give them a comical appearance. The weevil's 'nose' is properly called a rostrum and is not a nose at all as it carries the jaws at its end. Some weevils have disproportionately long rostrums, which leads to a great deal of head nodding, and their angled antennae add to the comic effect. Something else that endears me to weevils is the way many of them feed on the edges of leaves, cutting out neat, often very

symmetrically arranged, notches. However, this does not stop them being a big nuisance in the garden. The vegetable gardener is likely to notice the telltale notched leaves on his peas and beans in spring and summer, as the pea and bean weevil emerges to feed after overwintering among plant debris. I have also seen them chewing notches along the leaves of clover (a member of the pea family) in the lawn. It's nice to think that some of them are on your side.

Adult scrophularia weevils are small, about 2mm ($\frac{1}{12}$in) across, and resemble a knobbly grey-brown golf ball with a small patch of white, which makes them look like a small bird dropping – the ideal disguise against predators. You are likely to see these weevils on *Phygelius*, but most noticeable are their larvae and the damage that they cause. These are like tiny black slugs and produce, or cause the plant to produce, a black inky juice. They feed in shoot tips and among flower buds, distorting shoots and completely destroying the flowers.

The vine weevil is the bane of the container gardener. Fresh sterile compost used in planting up containers has none of the microscopic predatory nematodes that occur naturally in the soil and exert some control on the population. You can buy proprietary preparations of these nematodes for watering into the compost.

The vine weevil is a particularly troublesome pest, both indoors and out. A matt brownish-black creature with dull yellow spots and a deeply ribbed back or wing covers, it plods its way around the garden, most often after dark. Although it has wing covers, it does not fly.

All vine weevils are female, so no mating takes place. Each adult can lay between 100 to 1,000 eggs in a season, and of these approximately half are likely to develop. There is, therefore, considerable incentive to trap or collect and kill the adults where practical. Looking over your plants at night or checking under pots and debris in the glasshouse during the day and picking off the vine weevils can be a productive exercise. Alternatively, you can create a good daytime refuge for adults with a rolled-up piece of sacking or corrugated cardboard and then collect and kill them. The adults eat the leaves but it is the larvae that do the real damage. The white C-shaped grubs live in the soil and eat roots. They are easily spotted and anyone who has experienced vine weevil usually cannot wait to tell you how many they have found when they knocked their failing fuchsia or similar out of its pot. My best tally to date is 78 grubs from a single 25cm (10in) diameter pot.

Often the first indication of vine weevils being present is a wilting plant, in spite of wet compost or soil. If all the roots have been eaten away by the larvae, a gentle tug at the plant will bring it out of the ground. There seems little that these pests won't eat. Check out any sick-looking heucheras or houseleeks (*Sempervivum*), which are a favourite food outdoors. Indoors they love to eat their way up the fleshy stems, as well as the roots, of begonias and echeverias.

Development of the larvae depends on temperature, and outdoors usually only one generation is produced each year, with the larvae overwintering in the soil. In a conservatory or glasshouse, several generations and all stages – egg, larvae, pupae and adults – can be present at the same time (see page 100 for how to deal with them using biological controls).

It is the survival tactic of many insects, including weevils, to just drop off the plant when alarmed, so if you're after adult weevils, go armed with a sheet of newspaper to put under the bush or branch to catch them as they fall.

Mites

These form a large group of mostly very small creatures – a 2mm/1⁄12in long mite is a big one. (As I mentioned earlier, mites are not true insects and, consequently, they do not always respond to the same chemical treatments that control insects.) In the garden, mites play an important role in breaking down leaf litter and sustaining a healthy microfauna in the soil.

The red spider mite is among the less desirable species of mite. It loves the dry warm interior of a house and is the scourge of houseplants. At just over 0.5mm (1⁄50in) in length, this small mite is difficult to see and becomes obvious only when the plant growth becomes distorted, a fine bronzy speckling of tiny feeding marks appears on the upper leaf surface or a fine protective webbing is visible on the undersurface.

Less damaging from an ornamental point of view but more interesting in their effect are gall mites. Although the mites themselves are small and difficult to see, the galls that they create on stems and leaves are quite obvious. Nail galls, for example, are upright, narrowly conical growths that form on the leaves of lime trees; there is a smaller version that grows on sycamore leaves. Nail galls are often conspicuously red and can be so dense as to change the texture of the leaf surface completely. So-called witches brooms (the tangled growth sometimes mistaken for a bird's nest) seen among the branches of willow and birch are also a result of gall mite infection, which causes the tree to develop masses of twiggy growth at one spot.

Gall wasps

Equally noticeable are the galls caused by gall wasps, which are unrelated to gall mites. These cause curious red and green mossy pincushion-like growths on roses. Oaks are particularly prone to attack from several different types of gall wasp. The marble gall wasp causes one of the most noticeable galls: the wasp lays its eggs in an oak bud in spring, which causes the development of a smooth spherical gall about 25mm (1in) across. In its centre is a single larva. The adult emerges from the gall in autumn, and it is possible to see the exit hole. These galls persist on the tree for many years, looking to all intents and purposes like a part of the tree.

FUNGAL DISEASES

Where do we see them in the garden? The answer is everywhere, and what a varied lot they are! Obvious examples are toadstools, but you may have also seen bracket fungi standing out shelf-like on tree trunks, and the pink pustules of coral spot on dead twigs and branches. You're probably also famililar with black spot and mildews on roses, the grey mould that rots bunches of grapes and lettuce plants, and the bright orange rust pustules on the leaves and stems of roses. Even though these are all plant pathogens, you cannot help but appreciate the variety of shape and colour that exists among them. Many fungal diseases are visually very attractive, and a close look with a hand lens makes them even more so.

The effects of fungal diseases on plants vary greatly. Some can be devastating: Dutch elm disease, for example, which eventually kills the tree, is caused by a fungus; others can be just irritating, such as rust on ornamental willows, which is far from life threatening but you could definitely do without its seasonal blight. Fortunately, such fungal diseases pose no health threat to humans.

There is beauty in decay. The pink spore-bearing pustules of the common fungus coral spot (*Nectria cinnabarina*) are in evidence year round, but it is in winter that they stand out best among the gloom of wet leaves and decaying debris. Coral spot usually infects only dead wood but it can spread to live tissue.

Naming and shaming

For those who enjoy jargon, fungi can be split into three groups: saprophytes (living only on dead matter), facultative parasites (living on dead or living matter) and obligate parasites (living entirely on live matter). Almost all are characterized by microscopic filaments called hyphae, which form into a mass called a mycelium – this is what you get if you buy a 'grow your own mushrooms' pack.

Fungal diseases do not spread by producing seed but by spores – the brown dust that falls from an open mushroom if you stand it on the kitchen table. There are several families of fungi, and each one has a characteristic spore. Individually each fungus produces different types of spore through its life cycle, some sexual, some asexual. Some are particularly tough and designed for overwintering, while others also produce compact masses of mycelium to see them through the winter. For example, *Puccinia graminis* is a rust fungus with two alternate hosts, *Berberis* and wheat, and it produces no less than five different types of spore.

Above Usually, virus-infected plants are best destroyed but because of its ornamental value this virus-infected *Abutilon pictum* 'Thompsonii' is not just tolerated but actively propagated. The virus moves in the sap and can be introduced to related varieties by grafting them on to this rootstock. This gives rise to other combinations of leaf and flower colour.

Far right *Tulipa* 'Flaming Parrot' must surely be one of the most flamboyant of flowers. A virus suppresses the overlying red colour, allowing the base colour of yellow to show.

A brief look at the lifecycle of a common fungus will give you an idea of how complex they can be, and you will be probably be amazed at their ability to survive, reproduce and infect.

Let's start with an onion leaf infected with onion downy mildew, a widespread disease of onions and shallots, which is a particular nuisance when it's cold and wet. The spores of the fungus reveal themselves on the surface of the leaf as an off-white mildew. When the spores break free, dispersed by wind or water, they land on another onion leaf, where they germinate. Each spore then grows a tube that enters the leaf via one of the many thousands of stomata in the leaf. (Remember that this is all happening at a microscopic level.) This spore then infects the leaf and the whole lifecycle of the fungus starts again. As the decaying leaves drop to the ground, the disease enters the soil where it can survive for five years. Any seedlings that push up through the soil are infected with the disease, starting the process all over again. This illustrates the value of rotating your crops in the vegetable garden.

VIRUSES

At the risk of demoralizing anyone trying to identify a plant problem, the symptoms of virus infection can be a number of things and can appear in any combination: reduced vigour, chlorotic (pale) spots and blotches and patterning on leaves, reduced flowering, distorted flowers, yellowing leaf veins, and stunted and deformed leaves can all indicate virus attack. Unfortunately, these are all similar to symptoms caused by fungal diseases and insects. The viruses themselves are invisible, even under a microscope, which means that they are recognizable only by the symptoms that plants exhibit. Some plants carry a virus but show no symptoms at all, and it is only when that virus is carried to another plant that the symptoms become apparent.

Viruses are spread by insects, particularly aphids, and to a limited extent by seed and by infected sap on gardening tools such as secateurs and knives. They can overwinter in plant debris and survive several years in the soil. To add further to the gloom, there are no treatments available that will rid plants of viruses.

There is some hope, though. Some plants that show the effects of virus are actually welcome as ornamental plants in the garden: for example, the variegated Japanese honeysuckle (*Lonicera japonica* 'Aureoreticulata') and the yellow- and green-patterned leaves of the showy *Abutilon pictum* 'Thompsonii'. A virus causes the 'flaming' in certain tulip varieties that greatly increased the value of many tulips during the Dutch 'Tulipomania' of the 1630s.

Also encouraging is that virus-free plants and resistant varieties are available and should be bought when possible. Most of these are fruit and vegetable varieties because they are commercially valuable crops, but increasing numbers of virus-free ornamentals are available, too.

What can the gardener do about viruses? Unfortunately, as no viricides are available, good garden hygiene, as ever, is vital. That means not buying stunted or unhealthy looking plants. Buy plants and bulbs from trusted and reliable suppliers. Remove crop debris from the vegetable garden – weeds can harbour viruses, too. You also need to control insect pests as well as you can. Destroy any plants that look diseased, even if you're unsure as to whether the symptoms are caused by a virus. The plants affected by viruses are usually herbaceous or small shrubby plants, so it is not a major expense to get rid of them and replace them. Better safe than sorry.

COMING TO THE RESCUE

A natural plant ecology is mixed and diverse, which accounts for the general balance between plants and harmful insects. Any fluctuations in insect population usually sort themselves out over the years. But when we start growing plants in great swathes or monocultures, as we do in, say, wheat fields, the diversity is lost. It is then easy for a specific insect to make the most of this soft target without competition or predators, and for fungal spores to travel quickly from host to host. Man has to exert some control through spraying or by some other means.

While the garden is far from being a monoculture, we as gardeners are to some extent regularizing and taming nature. On top of that we introduce exotic species and hybrids whose resistance to indigenous pests and diseases is not the same as plants native to the area or country. Another point to bear in mind is that, although we may tolerate mildews on oak and rusts on willows in a natural landscape, we are unlikely to want similar diseases on our garden plants. To this end, chemical sprays have been, and still are being, developed.

Chemical controls

There are many different types of pesticide, and as new ones come and old ones go, it would be less than useful to list any of them here. Instead, what is more important is to understand how your chosen pesticide works so that you can make sure that you are using it most effectively.

Contact pesticides rely on the chemical solution actually hitting the quarry, so, in order for it to be effective, thoroughness is essential. Many contact pesticides are of short persistence and if you miss the target, such as an insect, it lives to feed another day. The fact that contact pesticides break down rapidly is an advantage when used on food crops because they leave no toxic residues.

With systemic treatments, the chemical is taken in by the leaves and moved around within a plant's system to kill insects or diseases wherever they may be. The theory sounds great, but it still means that you have to be thorough with the application because the crucial factor is how big a dose the insect receives. You cannot spray the lower leaves of a tree and expect the chemical to be carried in sufficient strength right through the tree, but you still have a chance of killing the pest or disease if you manage to cover most parts of the plant. Systemic treatments stay longer in the plant than contact insecticides.

Some composts have systemic insecticides mixed into them, providing protection for a whole season. You cannot use these composts for growing food crops, though, because the insecticide will be in every part of the plant, including what you harvest and eat.

Cultural and biological controls

The alternatives to the chemical control of pests and diseases are methods that rely on cultural and biological controls.

Cultural control is fundamental. It involves growing plants as healthily as possible, so that they are able to withstand whatever they might be confronted with. It is about being vigilant and looking out for pests and diseases before they get established. Rubbing off insects or removing infested leaves or shoots or pinching out infected shoots can reduce the build-up of the pest or disease, and rich pickings can be had from nighttime expeditions with the aim of collecting slugs, snails and vine weevils.

In essence, cultural control is good gardening and plant husbandry. It is growing varieties resistant to disease, maintaining a healthy and fertile soil, and cleaning and sterilizing your greenhouse regularly. It is also about tidying up decaying vegetation and plant debris in the vegetable garden to deny pests their overwintering sites and reduce sources of disease infection. In addition, it is important to grow as diverse a range of plants as possible, taking your roses out

Mealy bugs are a particular nuisance on indoor plants, and their waxy coating makes them difficult to eradicate by spraying. Biological control offers a good alternative. A ladybird relative called *Cryptolaemus* eats the eggs, as well as the young and adult mealy bug.

of the rose-bed monoculture and dispersing them among other shrubs and perennials, and getting rid of plants that persistently get infected with disease and pests – there go the roses altogether!

Biological control is the use of natural insect predators, parasites and bacteria to control harmful insects and diseases. It has come about for two reasons. First, the continual use of the same pesticides has allowed pests to build up a resistance to them, and an alternative was needed. Second, there is now a greater awareness of what is in our food and the effect that soil and plant treatments have on the environment. The public has made it clear that it does not want chemical residues in its food or the environment.

As is often the case, the major developments for the gardener come as a result of spin-offs from the commercial grower. Despite shelves full of bug killers and the like at garden centres, the domestic garden market for pesticides is tiny compared to that of the commercial sector, and as such warrants little research. Intensive cropping schedules, high temperatures and the rapid turnover of insect populations meant that glasshouse crop growers were the first to encounter pesticide-resistance problems. Fortunately, the warm enclosed environment of a glasshouse lent itself to the release of exotic flying predators to help control what were often exotic pests, and the results could be monitored. (I use the word 'exotic' in the sense of being from a foreign country rather than being flamboyant.) Subsequent developments have led to the introduction of many more control insects and nematodes (microscopic, thread-like worms) to deal with a wider range of pests.

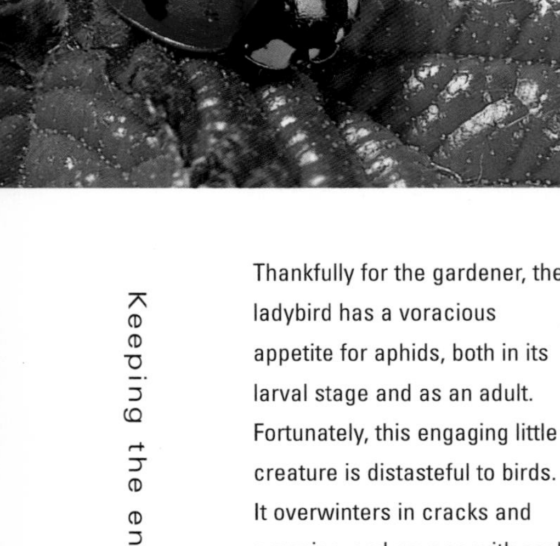

Thankfully for the gardener, the ladybird has a voracious appetite for aphids, both in its larval stage and as an adult. Fortunately, this engaging little creature is distasteful to birds. It overwinters in cracks and crannies, and anyone with sash windows may have come across quite large colonies huddled together inside the sash frame.

Very often the control insects already exist in the environment but in insufficient numbers to be effective. By rearing them artificially, they can be introduced in greater numbers than they occur naturally. For example, the nematode used to control vine weevils occurs naturally in the soil and is, to some extent, a controlling factor in the wild population, but in a sterile compost with no natural enemies it has a free run. (Not all nematodes are beneficial; some, like stem and bulb eelworms, distort and kill a wide range of garden plants.) One advantage of using nematodes as a control is that they will actively search out their prey by 'swimming' through the water held between soil particles.

Other examples of biological control include predatory midge larvae and parasitic wasps, which prey on adult aphids, and a fungus that infests them. Caterpillars can be kept at bay with bacteria, red spider mites with predatory mites, whitefly with parasitic wasps, and a fungus and mealy bug with a gruesome predatory beetle, which looks very much like the mealy bug itself but does not harm the plant.

Most of these biological controls work best in, and are most suited to, warm environments such as a greenhouse or conservatory and this is often where populations of pests build up rapidly. It is ironic, though, that before you can

introduce biological controls you need a population of a pest, so that the control insect has something to feed on. You will also have to tolerate a certain continued level of the pest insect to maintain the control population.

Outside in the garden you can use a combination of organic and biological methods of pest control, such as boosting the population of natural predators of insect pests. For example, you can increase the lacewing population by using pheromones (sex hormones), available from garden centres or by mail order, to attract them to a dry, bird-proof box at the end of autumn so that they overwinter safely. Contact treatments such as insecticidal soap will help to control pest numbers when there is a specific pest outbreak. (Insects breathe through pores in their skin which the fatty acids in the soap block up, so the insect dies.)

There are several species of lacewing, and both adults and larvae feed on aphids. Do not despair if you fail to see them in the garden; many of them are nocturnal, hiding during the day and coming out to feed at night.

You can also use pheromones to attract and trap the male codling moth, a pest of apples, and the plum fruit moth, thereby preventing breeding and reducing the pest population. Concentrated packs of a naturally occurring slug-feeding nematode are also available. Mixed with water they are applied to the soil where the microscopic nematodes seek out the slugs and kill them.

Don't forget that nature is already doing her bit to help. Hoverfly larvae can eat around 600 aphids before becoming adults; a ladybird can eat 4–6,000 aphids in its lifetime; a pair of great tits will feed 7–8,000 caterpillars to their brood; and a song thrush will consume up to 10,000 caterpillars, snails and grubs in its lifetime. Think twice before you buy that cat!

Relying on organic and biological controls outdoors is to some extent an act of faith. It is not easy to quantify the effects, and it is not always possible to say how things might have been if you had not used these methods of control. How can you really tell that there are more lacewings or fewer aphids in your garden than before? However, by making these controls part of your garden ethos and accepting that you will never completely rid your garden of pests or disease, you will have the satisfaction of knowing that your own environment is as untainted and as safe as you can make it.

WEEDKILLERS

Controlling weeds can take up a good part of the gardener's time and while I would rather not use chemical treatments in the garden, there are occasions when time constraints or simply the size of the task make weedkillers the only reasonable option.

There seems to be considerable misunderstanding about weedkillers and how they do their job, so I have divided them into groups according to how they work and suggested where each type may be used.

The way in which a weedkiller works is not always explained on the packaging, but if you know what method of action you want, then you have a basis for requesting a specific type of weedkiller, if not a specific product. Understanding what you want your weedkiller to do, knowing its limitations and the risks involved and being able to use it safely are the important things.

There are weedkillers available that combine several chemicals covering the three different types of action described below, but before you apply them, make sure that you understand exactly what they can do and whether they are really suitable for your needs.

Pre-emergent weedkillers

These either prevent the weed seed germinating or kill it as it germinates. Applied as granules or as a liquid, they are ideal for gravel paths and drives, as well as between paving slabs, because they bind to soil particles and stay in the

Given these statistics, what chance does the poor plant have at the base of every food chain? Fortunately, plants know a thing or two about surviving: plant material still makes up 99 per cent of the world's biomass (the total weight of the world's animal and plant population).

Those millions of insects and animals do not all eat living plant material and those that do, do not all kill the plants they feed on. A large proportion does not interfere with garden plants and some are even beneficial. Better still, some insects feed on the insects that feed on garden plants, and these are proving to be useful allies in the control of pests without chemicals (see page 100). Nor are all fungi out to destroy plants. Again, some of them are extremely important to plants and form close partnerships that benefit both plant and fungus. But the most important factor is that plants are resilient survivors and able to cope with almost anything nature throws at them – after all, they have been doing it for millions of years.

It would be intriguing to be able to go back in time and look at plants at, say, every half a million years to see how far their defences had developed. We could also see the see-sawing between a plant developing a defence strategy and the insect pest coming up with a way around it, only to prompt the plant to produce a different toxin or another change in its defences. This constant battle of readjustment is still going on, but such is the time scale of these gradual developments that we don't notice it. That insects are able to develop resistance to toxins is without doubt because several species of common garden and greenhouse pests have done just that. Within a relatively short time, the continued use of one type of insecticide has led to resistant strains of insects making that particular chemical useless. In evolutionary terms this has happened in the blink of an eye. Resistance to fungicides and even some herbicides has also developed for the same reason of over-use.

HOW PLANTS DEFEND THEMSELVES

Unlike animals, plants cannot run away from would-be predators, but it would be a mistake to think that they just sit there waiting to be eaten. They have a trick or two up their sleeves, and quite complicated ones at that.

The spines on *Pyracantha* and hawthorn, and the stinging hairs on nettles are outward signs that plants can defend themselves against larger grazing and browsing animals. But, apart from protective hairs, there are few visible signs of a plant being active in its battle against smaller pests and diseases. Because the defence mechanisms are internal and discrete, it is easy to underestimate how sophisticated they are.

An obvious way for a plant to defend itself against being eaten is to make its leaves, stems or fruit unpalatable or toxic, in the hope that one bite will be enough to discourage or even kill the attacking pest or animal. An example is yew (*Taxus baccata*): the foliage and the seeds in the red berries are lethal to even

Far left High levels of silica in the stems of horsetails (*Equisetum*) prevent weedkillers penetrating the plant. Raking or knocking the stem with a fork will bruise it sufficiently to allow some weedkiller in. It will take several applications to rid your garden of this pernicious weed.

Below It is no good pulling out dandelions unless you remove all of the taproot. Any root left will have the energy to send up new shoots and start all over again. A systemic weedkiller will travel to all parts of the plant and kill it completely.

Floral sex

A quiet affair

All is peaceful in the summer garden, except for the soft buzzing of insects. No grunting and groaning, no sweating or huffing and puffing because, when it comes to sex, plants are just not like that. For most plants, procreation is a quiet affair, though they are more than happy to get a third party involved, and for many of them it is absolutely essential that they do.

A group of large white flowers of *Lilium regale* attract insects from afar. As they get closer to the lilies, the flowers' sweet scent and markings on the petals guide the insects towards the nectar-bearing parts.

The *raison d'être* of every living organism is to reproduce, and plants are no exception. Plants have been around longer than most creatures – you can't have a plant-eating dinosaur unless it has some herbage to eat – and they have evolved a fascinating range of techniques for fertilization, some incredibly complicated, others extremely simple.

It is probably a while ago now since most of us studied biology, and memories of sepals, calyxes, anthers, perianths and the like have long since faded. Being told that a stamen (the male part) was made up of a filament and an anther, and the pistil (the female part) comprised a stigma, style and an ovary somehow seemed to make flowers unduly complicated. As a gardener I find it much easier to understand plant reproduction by actually looking at a flower whose individual components are large enough to be seen clearly.

There are a hundred and one more terms used to describe the various parts of the flower, but to be able to understand the basic elements, you need know only a few. These elements exist in one form or another in virtually every flower.

ON CLOSE EXAMINATION

We are all familiar with the spectacular florist's lily and have at some time managed to brush masses of orange pollen all over our clothes. These outsized open flowers, and similarly any large tulip flowers, have a simple structure, which makes it easy to see the important parts of the plant's reproductive system – ideal for some basic botany.

Let's look at the lily. Take one in your hand and study it closely while enjoying the scent. Then gently take the flower apart by pulling back and snapping off the petals (lilies usually have six). What are now exposed are the long stalks with orange or yellow canoe-shaped bits (these are usually black blobs in tulips) at the end. The stalks are the filaments (characteristically, lilies have six of these, too), the long 'canoes' are the anthers, and the orange 'dust' they produce, the pollen, much cursed by hay fever sufferers.

In freshly opened flowers the anthers will be sealed but as the flower matures, the anthers split along their length and unfold to release the ripe pollen. The transfer of this pollen, in effect the male sperm, to the female parts of another flower is the very crux of the plant's existence and the sole purpose of a flower. There are several ways in which the pollen can find its way to its intended flower but all of them are at the mercy of external agents. Before we explore the methods of pollen distribution let us look at the rest of the flower.

Down the centre of the flower is a long, tube-like structure, which is swollen at the top, and fatter and ribbed towards the base of the flower. The swollen tip is called the stigma, the tube is known as the style and the fat lower part is the ovary where the egg cells wait to be fertilized. It is easy to see that the ovary is split into three, long paired sections – these are destined to become the seed pod. The purpose of the stigma and style is to collect pollen at the sticky tip and nourish it with sugars and other chemicals so that it grows, and to guide each elongating pollen grain down the style to fertilize an egg cell. Each pollen grain is microscopic and when it lands on a stigma it starts to grow, putting out a tube that develops on the stigma and grows all the way down the style to the ovary;

Far left The complex looking but readily seen sexual parts of the passion flower (*Passiflora*) are said to represent the story of Christ's Passion and give the plant its name. The three stigmas represent the three nails, the five anthers the five wounds, and the five sepals and five petals stand for the ten apostles.

Centre *Fritillaria imperialis* also has a religious story attached to it. It was said to be the only plant not to bow its head at Christ's crucifixion and was made to weep and hang its flowers in shame ever since. Its 'tears' are drops of copious nectar that drip from the 'eyes' at the base of the petals.

Left The pollen-collecting stigma and long style are a prominent feature of *Crocus tournefortii*. It was the style of another crocus, *Crocus sativus*, that formed the basis of the once thriving European and Asian saffron industry. The styles were harvested and sold as a flavouring and dye.

in some plants this can mean a length of several centimetres. The silky hairs that you see growing in a tassel at the top of a sweet corn cob are styles and, in order for each individual corn to swell, a pollen grain has to germinate at the tip of that silky hair and produce a tube that grows all the way down to fertilize the single corn at its end. It's an amazing feat.

Occasionally the styles or filaments develop into petal-like structures, giving rise to flowers with apparently many more petals than usual. These are the ornamental double flowers we see so often in the garden. Many of them are sterile which, bearing in mind the origin of these extra petals, is not surprising since they are no longer able to function as reproductive organs.

FLYING ON THE WIND

The simplest but most hit-and-miss way of pollen reaching another flower is for it to be set free on the wind and blown to the next bloom. With this strategy, a great deal of pollen misses its target completely and is wasted, so plants that use this method of propagation, such as most grasses and a number of trees, produce vast quantities of pollen to reduce the odds. If you take a close look at the flowers of wild grasses, you will see that each head of grass is made up of many small flowers. You'll also notice the pollen-bearing anthers, which are held out and waggle quite freely to allow maximum disturbance by the wind, and the feathery stigmas filtering the wind for pollen. Hay fever sufferers are all too aware of the warm and windy conditions ideal for the greatest release of pollen.

Wind-pollinated flowers do not need to waste valuable resources on attracting insects, so they do not sport showy petals or produce attractive scents. Instead they have anthers that are prominently exposed to the wind and stigmas well adapted to catch the pollen.

Because of their height the flowers on trees are ideally positioned to have their pollen carried on the wind. The early spring flowers of the Italian alder (*Alnus cordata*) and hazel (*Corylus avellana*) are good examples of this. Their long catkins are ideally designed for casting pollen to the breeze and, if you look carefully along the branches of the hazel, you will see small red tufts which are the feathery stigmas waiting to catch the pollen. (The corkscrew hazel, *Corylus avellana* 'Contorta', with its contrasting twisted stems and sharply vertical catkins is particularly effective.) Male yew flowers also put out considerable amounts of pollen; shake a bough to see drifts of it fall from the catkins. Birches, alders, walnuts, poplar, oaks and sweet chestnuts all bear catkins; some are long and ornamental, which adds another season of interest.

It is common for the male and female flowers to be separated on wind-pollinated plants. The pollen-bearing tassels on the common nettle (*Urtica dioica*) indicate that this plant, too, is pollinated by the wind, but in this case the male and female flowers are not only separate but grow on separate plants. Such plants are said to be dioecious. Greek scholars will tell you the word comes from *di* meaning two, and *oikia* meaning household. A dioecious plant has its female flowers on one plant and its male flowers on another. There are several common garden plants, including holly (*Ilex*), yew (*Taxus*) and willow (*Salix*), that are dioecious. The scientific names of some plants, such as goat's beard (*Aruncus dioicus*), reflect this feature. A monoecious plant is one that has separate male and female flowers on the same plant, such as the hazel.

With dioecious plants such as holly and willow, where each specimen will bear only male or female flowers, it is important to choose a female plant if you want berries, or male plants if you want catkins. No matter how much you feed a male holly and scare the birds from its boughs, it will never produce berries. To confuse

Far left The male flowers of hazels are the very obvious catkins hanging from the stems of *Corylus avellana* 'Contorta'. The female flowers are less obvious – look out for their little red, pollen-catching, bristly tufts further along the branch, where nuts will be produced.

Below *Aruncus dioicus*, as its name suggests, produces male and female flowers on separate plants. The male flowers are bigger and showier, although both sexes produce worthwhile displays.

the gardener, though, the holly varieties 'Silver Queen' and 'Golden Queen' are, in fact, male and will have no berries while 'Golden King' is a female holly and likely to carry a good crop of berries.

You should also try to get the right sex of other dioecious garden plants if you specifically want the ornamental berries or fruit. For example, *Aucuba japonica* is usually grown for its foliage, but many varieties have conspicuous large red berries; the male catkins of *Garrya elliptica* are longer than the female catkins; the sea buckthorn (*Hippophae rhamnoides*) has fleshy orange-red berries in winter but you will need a male nearby to pollinate and set the berries; the Osage orange (*Maclura pomifera*) produces its huge fruits only on the female; and you will need both male and female plants of *Actinidia deliciosa* if you want to produce Chinese gooseberries, or kiwi fruits.

POLLINATION BY INSECTS

Rather than relying on the wind for pollination, many plants have developed methods of spreading pollen by using insects. It almost goes without saying that because of the diverse nature of insects and the almost infinite adaptability of plants, a great number of techniques and adaptations have arisen for ensuring that the pollen gets to where it is needed. Some are very simple and open to a wide range of pollinators, while others are so geared to a specific insect that any threat to that insect's welfare also poses a threat to the plant. So what may be seen as a very complex and clever bit of evolution may in fact be running the plant up a blind alley.

Echinacea purpurea has flower heads made up of many tiny individual flowers, typical of plants in the daisy family. Bees forage for nectar among these flowers, picking up pollen as they go.

The aims of the plant are to attract the insect to the flower, get it to pick up some pollen and then carry it to another plant of the same type and deposit the pollen so that it fertilizes the embryo. That is the intention of every flower in your garden, although it would be nice to think that they were being pretty just for you.

The initial attraction is usually visual, though insects are known to pick up scents at low concentrations over long distances. The colour or conspicuous nature of the flower is what attracts the insect closer, then scent can play a stronger part. There has to be a reward for the insect visiting a flower and it is food in the form of nectar. Nectar is a sugar-rich substance, usually liquid, that insects feed on and some, like bees, use it to make honey. If you place one hand underneath the flower of a crown imperial (*Fritillaria imperialis*), for example, and tap the top of the flower with your other hand, drops of sweet nectar will fall into your palm. *Melianthus major* and *M. comosus* produce abundant ink-black nectar.

The plant hides its nectar deep in the flower so that an insect has to get right into the flower to find it, giving the plant plenty of opportunity to load the insect with pollen before it leaves for another flower. Some bees that visit runner bean flowers have got wise, however. Instead of pushing themselves down into the flower and past the pollen-bearing anthers, they approach it from the side and

make a hole straight to the nectary. Unfortunately, this bypasses the pollination process and so reduces the number of beans that the plant is able to produce.

Rather than waste energy by making a spectacle of every flower, some plants lure the insect with just a few large flowers around plainer looking ones. These showy flowers may even be sterile and act solely as attractants. This occurs on some viburnums and lace cap hydrangeas. Once the hydrangea flowers are fertilized, the showy sterile florets turn downwards so as not to draw insects away from the flowers that are still to be pollinated.

We must remember that insects do not see flowers as we do. They are more sensitive to ultraviolet light and, while we see patterns and lines such as the dots and blotches on foxglove flowers and striations on the iris and lily flowers, they see them more intensely and in a markedly different way from us. For example, some flowers that we see as plain white will look far more interesting to a bee, which sees the ultraviolet markings within the white. This raises the interesting

There are some incredibly complex mechanisms for ensuring pollination but *Magnolia stellata* has none of them. It relies on attracting insects with its glistening flowers, then letting them get on with it. It is this simplicity that gives the plant its beauty.

and rather philosophical point as to why we see flowers as things of beauty when they are not even designed for our eyes.

Plants have evolved various devices – some simple, others far more complicated – to ensure the insect picks up pollen from the anthers of one plant and deposits some on the sticky stigmas of others. Magnolias are considered rather primitive plants with relatively underdeveloped flowers that rely simply on the insect bumbling about in the flower for its propagation. Members of the *Salvia* family, on the other hand, use more sophisticated methods. The flowers of

The fertilized seeds then develop into large, bright red berries held on the upright stem (see page 117) and the spathe withers and falls away. No matter that it may have taken millions of years for this arum to develop such a complex structure and sequence of events, it still fills me with wonder.

Another way of discouraging self-fertilization is to have the reproductive parts arranged differently in different flowers. In primrose flowers, some have what looks like a pinhead in the centre, while others have nothing. These two different types of flower are called pin-eyed and thrum-eyed. In pin-eyed flowers the 'pinhead' at the opening of the flower is the pollen-receiving stigma at the tip of the style. The pollen-producing anthers are further down the flower. In thrum-eyed flowers the anthers are at the opening of the flower and the stigma lower down. This ensures that if an insect collecting pollen at one sort of flower goes to the same sort of flower, the pollen does not contact a stigma. However, if it visits the other type, the pollen is delivered to the receptive stigma, thus effecting cross-pollination. A further safeguard exists as each flower has antibodies that stop the development of pollen from itself or a like flower.

THE WEIRD AND THE WONDERFUL

Although not relevant to the average garden, it is difficult to resist giving other examples of incredible adaptations made by plants to effect pollination. The climber *Cobaea scandens* can be pollinated by bats, and there is one climbing member of the pea family whose flowers are also pollinated in this way. As the pollen and stigmas ripen, the 'standard' petals rise to form a concave shape that accurately reflects the bat's 'radar' signals. This lets the bat know exactly which flowers are ready to be visited. The good old indestructible aspidistra is pollinated by snails that crawl across the ground-level flowers.

Bees visiting certain plants belonging to the potato family beat their wings at the same low frequency as the anthers, which triggers a shower of pollen through a pore in the end of the anther. It is surely impossible to be blasé about such delightful details of natural design.

GIVING NATURE A HELPING HAND

New varieties are the lifeblood of commercial plant growers, particularly, it would seem, to rose and sweet pea growers come the time of the great horticultural exhibitions, such as the Chelsea Flower Show in London. Can there really be anything new left in the rose world?

One way of producing new varieties is by controlling the fertilization process. Two existing varieties are crossed with each other using the controlled transfer of pollen from one plant to another. There has to be no risk of the recipient female parent plant pollinating itself and, to be absolutely sure of this, the plant breeder carefully removes the anthers of an unopened bud a day or so before the flower opens, using a sharp knife to remove the petals and a needle to pick out the unwanted anthers. The flower is then isolated by sealing a paper bag around the bud to prevent cross-pollination by insects or the wind. The stigma is allowed to mature and then pollen from the chosen male parent is brushed on to the stigma before it is isolated again and left for around ten days, when the bag is removed and the seeds are allowed to develop. The resulting progeny are assessed for colour, scent, vigour, disease resistance, and so on.

THE SEED

There are so many awe-inspring aspects to plants that I am wary of going overboard about yet another, but I must say that the seed has to be one of the most miraculous features of a plant. It can be as fine as dust, as in *Begonia semperflorens* and orchids, as big and as obvious as a kidney bean or chestnut, and, if we go tropical, as impressive as a coconut. It will have been blown, launched, shot, washed, eaten or just dropped from its parent plant to end up who knows where and, with the survival of its species depending on it, it is expected to put out roots and shoots to establish itself as a new plant. Okay, I might have been a bit overdramatic about the survival of the species, but that seed doesn't know that it's not the only seed and it acts as though it is by giving itself the best chance of germinating.

'From tiny acorns do mighty oak trees grow', and from tiny sunflower seeds do mighty sunflowers grow. The bursting of the embryonic root and the rapid development of the seed leaves, all from the food stored in the seed, will always be one of the wonders of nature. All the information that will control a plant's height, shape, age, in fact every aspect of its growth, is bound in the genetic coding in its seed.

As inert as a seed may appear, it is able to detect moisture, oxygen and nutrient levels and the amount of light that exist outside its skin. Using this information, it decides when the conditions are right to germinate.

Seeds will not want to germinate if conditions are too cold, dry or hot, which would put the new plant at risk. (The ability to detect temperature variations may also be used by some seeds to tell how deep they are in the soil – the further down in the ground they are, for example, the smaller the variation in temperature between day and night.)

Seeds are also able to detect different intensities and qualities of light. Light penetrates the soil for a surprising distance, which could be up to several centimetres. Some seeds will not germinate if they are exposed to the light, which tells them that they are not buried and could be in an exposed and dangerous position. In what seems a contradictory strategy, other seeds will not germinate in the dark and need to sense light so that the new plant has the light to flourish in as it grows.

Some seeds need a period of cold before they will germinate, such as *Cotoneaster* and *Viburnum*, and others, like *Rosa*, contain inhibitors that need to be washed out before they germinate. Some plants produce seeds that stagger their germination over a period of months or years to increase the odds of at least some of them growing in favourable conditions. Unfortunately, the common weed groundsel (*Senecio vulgaris*) is one of them.

Fortunately, the majority of commonly grown seeds germinate quite readily without much help from us but, for some, you may need to reproduce their growing conditions in the wild. You might have to chill the seeds in the fridge, store them in compost outdoors so that they experience the effects of bacteria, fungus and of cold and rain, or give them periods of heat before chilling. Some seeds have a hard coating that is a physical barrier to their germination, which won't take place until the coating has been degraded by bacteria over a period of months. The seeds of *Canna* and *Alstroemeria*, for example, benefit from having some of the hard outer coating chipped away before sowing, as this lets in water and oxygen to trigger the development of the seed's embryo.

Bane or beauty? With its great pink spires of flowers finished, the willowherb (*Epilobium angustifolium*) has set seed. As it dries out, the seed capsule starts to split and curl back to reveal the mature seed. The familiar seed will fluff out its 'parachute' and launch itself on the wind to travel just yards or maybe miles to establish another colony.

For many seeds there is no one factor that guarantees germination and it is often the interaction of a range of conditions that brings the seed to the point of sprouting.

SEED DISPERSAL

Before botanists get too hot under the collar, I must point out that I am using the word 'seed' fairly loosely here, to avoid bombarding you with a whole string of interesting but daunting botanical terms.

Having spent much energy on attracting pollinators, producing pollen, moving the pollen from plant to plant and then producing a seed, a plant still has one more hurdle to overcome. And in doing so, I am glad to say that nature does not let us down; there seem to be as many ingenious devices and cunning adaptations to ensure efficient seed dispersal as there are ways to ensure that the seed is fertilized in the first place.

If you pause beneath poplar trees on a breezy early summer day and gaze up, you will see shreds of cloud being blown from the ends of the branches. Look around you at the heaps of this dirty white 'candyfloss' whisked and blown into every corner and catching on roughened surfaces. If you take a handful of this airy fluff and tease it apart, you'll find the small seeds buried within. It is hard to imagine that the large poplar standing next to you came from such a downy speck. Small as the seed is, it still needs its coat of fluff to give it sufficient resistance to the wind, and to act as a parachute carrying it great distances on summer thermals.

There are other plants that disperse their seed to the wind. If you have ever gardened next to wasteland or an abandoned allotment, you will undoubtedly have cursed the great clouds of seed blowing from stands of willowherb (*Epilobium angustifolium*). Then there are the self-set willows that produce fluffy seeds that blow in ready to set young willows in your patch, and dandelions that, despite pretty images of their seeds blowing across buttercupped meadows, you still cannot bring yourself to love. The fat poker-like heads of the greater reedmace break up in the autumn, spilling their seeds to the wind and water in their efforts to stifle every waterway.

But enough of these 'weeds'; there are plenty of wind-borne seeds that offer pleasure rather than gloom. Think of the spinning helicopters that fall from the sycamore tree, miniature masterpieces of aerodynamics, and the ungainly and slightly comical flight of seeds from lime trees.

Some seeds have hairs to catch the wind, and these can be ornamental like those of many clematis species. The vigorous yellow-flowered *Clematis* 'Bill Mackenzie' puts on a very good show of silvery silken tassels that persist for several months. Each clematis seed is like a tadpole with a very elongated tail covered in silky hair. This gives the seed the necessary surface area to be caught by the wind and blown away as it falls from the plant. Orchid seeds are so tiny that they can be carried by the wind without any plumes or wings. Their size means that they carry no reserves of energy and have insufficient food to begin growth on their own. To germinate they rely on being penetrated by a fungus, which they use to obtain nutrients.

Some common garden plants are dispersed by the wind but by less obvious means. Love-in-a-mist (*Nigella*) and *Lychnis* rely on the wind buffeting and bending their stems to shake out their seeds, as does the poppy. If the weather is damp, internal flaps close the holes around the top of the poppy seed head where the seeds come out, keeping them dry for better distribution another time.

Unlike flowers or fleshy edible seeds, wind-borne seeds are not designed to be attractive to insects or birds, so their beauty is all ours. The silky tassels of clematis seed make fluffy pompoms, many of which last well into winter, giving the plant another season of interest.

If your dog returns from a walk in the country with burdock seeds in its fur, you will know only too well of another means of dispersing seeds. Burdock (*Arctium minus*), of dandelion and burdock fame, forms rounded burs of hooked seeds that latch on to animal fur. The seeds are then carried until the animal grooms them out or they eventually break up and come away.

Hooked seeds occur on several species in the garden. The low ground-cover plant *Acaena* has heads of hooked seeds, and as you weed the border you might notice the seed heads of certain species of *Geum* sticking to your sleeves or trousers. Another common plant with hooked seeds, but this time a weed, is cleavers (*Galium aparine*), which, surely, must have been designed for schoolboys to play with – its small round seeds are covered in hooks that will stick to almost any clothing but they are ideal for getting tangled in woolly jumpers. This plant has always been a source of wonder to me. It makes a substantial, clambering, sprawling and smothering mass of narrow hooked stems, but if you trace it back to the ground, it seems impossible that the single almost hairlike stem could supply all that greenery with the water and nutrients necessary for survival.

The hooked seeds of burdock are very efficient at latching on to animals. Once attached to its 'transport', the seed is carried around until it breaks down and falls free or is groomed out by the animal.

Sitting in the garden on a hot day you may hear the occasional crack or pop coming from broom (*Cytisus scoparius*) plants. This is caused by the seed pods drying out but with each half of a pod doing so at a different rate until, suddenly, the two halves spring apart with a twist, flinging the seeds some considerable distance. That's not the complete story of seed dispesal, however; the seeds are frequently carried away by ants, which find the outer coating nutritious but leave the seed untouched.

Broom and gorse are not the only plants to use a vigorous method of dispersing their seeds. Even more explosive are the 'cucumbers' of the squirting cucumber *Ecballium elaterium*. It is a low-growing hardy plant and, although not particularly showy, it is easy to grow from seed and well worth doing so for its impressive seed-shooting capabilities alone. The squat, gherkin-like cucumber hangs vertically from a short upright stem but as it nears ripeness, it lifts up 45 degrees. Its internal pressure builds up until it is high enough for the fleshy cucumber to break away from the stem and to squirt out its seeds with phenomenal velocity. I have known them carry for 3m (10ft) or more. You can set them off yourself with a gentle touch when they are ready to go, but stand well back from the line of fire and mind your eyes.

The Himalayan balsam (*Impatiens glandulifera*), a very large relative of the busy Lizzie, sits awkwardly between being a weed and a garden ornamental. It is a robust annual that gets to 2.5m (8ft) high in a very short time but its fascination is that it has exploding seed pods that send the small hard seeds flying all over the place. Once you have discovered it, try stopping yourself touching the seeds to trigger them; it's like trying not to scratch an itch.

Two much more common garden plants also have what the botanists call 'active ballistic mechanisms' for seed dispersal. The mechanism of *Geranium pratense* is not only efficient but also elegant. When the pointed seed heads are sufficiently dessicated, they split into five strips that rapidly curl back to the outermost tip and, in doing so, fling the seeds from a tiny cup attached to the end of each strip. The strips come to rest and sit like a crown at the top of the seed head. Easier to miss but appealing in their detail are the seed pods of violas, which open to reveal what look like three tiny canoes. As the open seed pods dry out, they squash the hard shiny seeds together until, under pressure, they shoot out.

Unfortunately, weeds have got in on the act, as anyone who has tried to weed out the annual hairy bittercress knows. This small plant sends seeds flying from their long narrow pods at the slightest touch, guaranteeing another good crop.

Dishing the dirt

What lies beneath

Have you ever wondered what lies beneath your feet as you stand in your garden? There are thousands of metres of a whole mix of geological deposits; layers that have been heaved and shifted, bent and twisted as the earth's crust settled down.

Over the millions of years that the Earth has been in existence, it has been continually battered by wind and rain, scorched by blazing sun, pounded by the sea and rent by frost, ground by glaciers and dissolved by acidic rain. Little by little, this has chipped away at the rocky surface, grinding it into ever-smaller mineral particles that constitute the basic elements of soil. It is difficult to imagine that millions of tons have been eroded by these simple mechanical processes and that they have been deposited in layers many metres thick. Just what those particles are made of will depend on the rock they came from. They are not necessarily from the underlying bedrock; glaciers from the Ice Age or rivers may have carried sediment many hundreds of miles and mixed it with other types of rock before depositing it in your garden.

The fact that the Grand Canyon was once solid rock will give you an idea of the vast amounts of material moved. All that material has been washed downstream, to be deposited on flood plains, in deltas or carried out to sea; some may have been blown away from dry river banks to lie on ground miles away. Many areas that are now dry land were once covered by the sea.

Great layers of clay in the clay pit at a brick works, the hundreds of metres of chalk in the famous white cliffs of Dover and road cuttings with solid rock going down beyond the levels where roots might reach are all visible examples of the underlying layers of soil. It is these layers that give most soils their basic characteristics when it comes to drainage and alkalinity (see page 130). But just to show that there are no hard and fast rules, not far from my alkaline limestone garden is a garden with a small natural patch of acidic soil that grows, most incongruously, rhododendrons. So, do not expect your garden to be the same all over; it can change within half a metre or so.

The underlying geology of our gardens is permanent, whether it is clay, chalk, like the white cliffs of Dover (opposite) or rock, like the Grand Canyon (right). But we can improve that relatively thin but very valuable layer of soil that skims the surface.

In undisturbed soils, weathering and decaying vegetation and animals, both large and microscopic, have over many hundreds of years caused the build-up of organic matter in the soil and so produced a stable structure that leaves you with the most nutritious soil near the surface. Topsoil can be a luxurious 60–80cm (2–2½ft) deep, or in poorer conditions only 1–2.5cm (½–1in).

Most of us garden on land that, while far from natural, has been cultivated for a good number of years and a topsoil has been established. We should maintain and improve this topsoil by treating it as nature would and applying a layer of organic matter each year.

Good soil is teeming with life, much of it microscopic, and there may be many millions of microorganisms in one gram of soil. In fact, there can be so many that a crumb of soil greater than 3mm (⅛in) across can be devoid of oxygen at its centre because of all the tiny organisms using it up. Soil is a resource to be treasured and nurtured. The squashing and smearing of soil with diggers and dumpers on building sites destroys in a day what may have taken hundreds of years to build up. Carting away most of the topsoil, leaving just enough to put a thin skim over the compacted land strewn with builders' rubble, is a deplorable waste and makes creating a garden difficult.

Opposite

1 *Camellia japonica*

2 *Kalmia latifolia*

3 *Hydrangea macrophylla*

4 *Enkianthus campanulatus*

WHAT KIND OF SOIL DO I HAVE?

We are often told that this plant thrives best on a sandy loam or that plant won't tolerate limy clay, but how do you know what soil you have in the garden? First of all, you determine the pH of your soil.

Soil pH

The pH of a soil is the measurement of its acidity or alkalinity, which, in crude terms, means how much lime it contains. (For the linguists among you, the term pH comes from the French *puissance d'hydrogène*, or strength of hydrogen.) Fortunately, there are several devices for testing a soil's pH available from garden centres. The simplest gadget is a probe that you push into the soil from which you take a reading. A slightly more laborious method, but one that makes you feel more of a boffin, involves little test tubes, along with various solutions and comparison charts.

Let's say that you choose the probe, and the reading might simply say acidic, neutral or alkaline, or give you an actual pH figure. The higher the pH figure, the limier the soil; the lower the pH, the more acidic. Pure water is taken as a neutral pH 7.0. Below that is acid, with pH 4.5–5.5 being very acid and the lower limit for nearly all plants. Above pH 7.0 is alkaline, or limy.

An easier, albeit crude way of determining the pH of your soil is to look around at your neighbours' gardens to see if they have healthy-looking *Rhododendron*, *Erica*, *Azalea* or *Pieris* growing (these are all plants of the large family Ericaceae, hence 'ericaceous plants'). If they do, then it's a safe bet that their soil – and yours – is acidic. While acid-loving plants will not grow on alkaline soil, the converse is not true, so a lack of ericaceous plants is not a sure sign of alkaline soil. However, if you see the likes of lilac, *Philadelphus* and *Hypericum*, plants that enjoy alkaline conditions, then a neutral to alkaline soil is quite possible.

Plants for acid soil

SOME OF THE SHOWIEST FLOWERING SHRUBS THRIVE ON ACID SOIL BUT THE LIST BELOW SHOWS THAT SOME VERY GOOD FOLIAGE PLANTS DO AS WELL.

Acer palmatum
Calluna
Camellia (1)
Cornus kousa
Embothrium
Enkianthus (4)
Fothergilla
Gaultheria cuneata
Gaultheria mucronata
Hydrangea macrophylla (3)
Kalmia latifolia (2)
Lapageria
Pieris
Rhododendron
Vaccinium

Plants for akaline soil

AS THIS LIST SHOWS, ALKALINE SOILS ALLOW THE GROWING OF A BROAD RANGE OF PLANTS THAT PROVIDE FLOWER AND FOLIAGE INTEREST OVER A VERY LONG SEASON

Berberis
Buddleja
Chaenomeles
Cotinus
Cotoneaster
Cytisus nigricans
Deutzia
Kolkwitzia amabilis (3)
Mahonia aquifolium
Osmanthus
Philadelphus
Phlomis fruticosus
Potentilla
Sambucus (4)
Syringa
Viburnum carlesii
Viburnum lantana
Viburnum opulus (1 and 2)
Weigela florida

WORKING WITH WHAT YOU HAVE

There is one very good reason to know what type of soil you have before setting off to the garden centre to buy your plants. If you have a soil that is limy, high alkaline or has a high pH (they all mean the same thing), there are some very showy and commonly offered plants that will not thrive in your garden (see list on page 131). If the plant label doesn't tell you that the plant can be grown in limy soil, be sure to find out before you buy. Any attempt to grow acid-loving plants in limy soil will result in them becoming pale and sickly.

So why does lime cause such a problem? It is all to do with the uptake of nutrients by the roots. In alkaline conditions iron becomes locked up in the soil and unavailable to the plant. Iron is a crucial element in the initial formation of the molecules of the green pigment chlorophyll. Chlorophyll gathers the sun's energy to fuel the plant. (An interesting aside is that the chemical structure of chlorophyll is very similar to a substance called haem, which is a component of haemoglobin, the oxygen-carrying element in blood. It does make you wonder whether there is a common origin.)

There are treatments you can apply to the soil or foliage that offer iron to the plant in different accessible forms (sequestered iron or iron chelate), but their effects are always temporary and they need to be repeated regularly. An alternative is to lower the pH of the soil by adding powdered sulphur, available from garden centres, which is broken down into sulphuric acid by bacteria, thus acidifying the soil.

But this is a battle you are never going to win. These are all temporary fixes and, rather than continually fight against nature, it is more convenient and natural to grow plants that suit your soil; they will be healthier and more vigorous. If you really must go against the flow, grow your acid lovers in pots.

Opposite

1 *Viburnum opulus*
2 *Viburnum opulus*
3 *Kolkwitzia amabilis*
4 *Sambucus*

HOW DOES IT FEEL?

It's likely you'll already have an idea whether your soil is particularly high in clay or sand by the way it behaves when wet, and as long as your plants grow well, that's probably all you'll need to know. However, in a new garden, you might like to know if your soil is going to drain well or be easy to work, and it is also useful to know if your soil is different in different parts of the garden. If I moved to a new garden, curiosity and the satisfaction of knowing would drive me to find out more about my soil. Here's how to do it.

The soil test

There is a fairly complex classification of soil textures but for the average gardener it is enough to know which of five categories your soil belongs to: sandy, light loam, silt, clay loam and clay. With the following test, you will, in effect, find out by feel (texture), the size of particles that your soil contains.

Sand has the largest particles, followed by silt, then clay, which has by far the smallest particles. (Loam is made up of sand, silt and clay; clay loam has a higher proportion of clay than light loam.) Please don't be put off by these unfamiliar terms, though; just get out into the garden and have a go.

Take an amount of soil a bit smaller than a golf ball, and knead it between your forefinger and thumb until you have broken down all the lumps. If necessary, add a little water to get it to stick together as much as it is likely to; if you have no water handy and no one is looking, a bit of spit will do. Then examine the soil and answer the following questions:

1 Is the moist soil predominantly sandy and does it feel very gritty?
If the answer is Yes, go to question 2. *If the answer is No, go to question 3.*

2 Is it difficult to roll the soil into a ball?
Yes. Your soil is **sandy**. No. Your soil is **light loam**.

3 Does it mould into an easily deformed ball and feel smooth and silky?
Yes. Your soil is **silt**. *If the answer is No, go to question 4.*

4 Does the soil mould to form a strong ball and does it smear but not take a polish when rubbed?
Yes. Your soil is **clay loam**. *If the answer is No, go to question 5.*

5 Does the soil mould to form a strong ball like plasticine, take a polish and feel sticky when wetter?
Yes. Your soil is **clay**.

A quicker but less accurate test of your soil texture is to prepare your soil as above then simply roll it into a sausage shape between your palms and try to join the ends together to make a circle. The easier it is to make the ends meet without the sausage breaking, the more clay there is in the soil.

SOIL STRUCTURE

Maintaining or developing a good soil structure goes a very long way towards growing healthy plants.

It can be said that the two extremes of soil texture – sand and pure clay – have no structure. Try running up a sand dune and you soon realize that there is nothing holding the sand together. Take a lump of solid clay and you know that there is very little chance of breaking it apart. In between these two extremes is a wide range of structures where the soil is broken up into crumbs and lumps of various sizes (peds is the technical name for these aggregates). These crumbs are held together by natural glues, which include clay and sticky substances produced by the millions of microbes in each small piece of soil. Good structure means an open soil with plenty of spaces for air and water to get in and for easy penetration by roots; 60 per cent of a good soil is pore space.

Clay soil

Is clay soil really the gardener's bane, as it is so often called? Well, yes and no. The majority of soils have some clay in them and it is a good job they do. You may well have heard gardeners with clay soil say that once established their plants grow very well and that their soil is very fertile. This is because the clay element plays a vital role in maintaining soil fertility, so it's better to cope with a slightly heavy soil than have no clay at all.

For the sake of simplicity, clay particles can be thought of as microscopic, rather flat dinner plates that will lie very close against each other with little space between them. If you could take a gram of clay and flatten it as thinly as you could – a rolling pin won't do – it would cover an area about 20 square metres (200 square feet)!

Anyone who has ever made pottery will know how slippery clay feels when it is on the wheel. That is because the plate-like particles slip very smoothly over one another. Because they fit so snugly together water cannot pass between them easily, hence the very slow-draining nature of clay soils. That is the bad news. The good news is that these particles carry an electric charge that makes them attract nutrients from the water in the soil, releasing them over a period of time through the action of microbes and chemical activity. This makes them potentially very fertile soils.

It is worth considering the value of these clay particles when buying compost for hanging baskets and containers. Purely organic composts like peat have no such particles and they are unable to retain any quantity of nutrients. Soil-based composts, on the other hand do contain clay particles and any feed you apply is going to stay in the compost a lot longer and not be washed out as quickly as it will be in a peat-based version.

Clay can hold a considerable amount of water between the particles. Because the soil contains such vast numbers of these particles, when water is lost after a prolonged dry spell, the soil shrinks by a surprising amount – you might not lose your wheelbarrow down them, but some cracks are certainly wide enough for your foot to fit into. These cracks obviously pull roots apart and cause damage but, ironically, they also improve natural drainage as plant litter falls into them and preserves a passageway when the ground swells again.

A problem you may have come across after you have carefully prepared a seed bed and sown a row of seeds is that clay soil becomes capped: it forms a hard surface crust that can be tough enough to prevent seedlings getting through.

Plants for clay soil

CLAY SOILS MAY PREVENT THE GROWING OF FINE-ROOTED WOODLAND PLANTS BUT THERE ARE STILL PLENTY OF GOOD PLANTS FOR CLAY, AS THIS LIST SHOWS.

Aucuba (2)
Cotinus coggygria (3)
Deutzia (1)
Pyracantha (6)
Ribes sanguineum (5)
Rubus biflorus
Rubus cockburnianus
Vinca major non-variegated (4)
Vinca minor

This also occurs on bare soil between plants, particularly in the winter. What has happened is the rain has battered the soil surface and settled the soil particles together, and the clay particles, being the smallest and flattest, get washed and pounded together to form a tough barrier. This also happens when you regularly water your containers in the same place; the water washes the soil together and it then takes ages for water to drain through the surface layer. In both cases a light organic mulch will reduce the action of the water and the capping effect.

Clay's ability to lock up chemicals is a useful process in rendering some herbicides harmless; for example, any Paraquat that misses the leaves and reaches the ground will be tied up by the clay particles. An antidote for anyone who mistakenly drank Paraquat was to eat fuller's earth – a form of clay that was at one time used extensively as cat litter!

Opposite

1 *Deutzia ningpoensis*
2 *Aucuba japonica*
3 *Cotinus coggygria*
4 *Vinca major*
5 *Ribes sanguineum*
6 *Pyracantha*

Sandy soil

Sandy soils are in many ways a dream: never sticky, free draining and you can work them very soon after rain. These qualities, however, bring their own problems. Sandy soils are extremely hungry and, because they are so free draining, they are very dry. It is a curious thing that the two extreme ends of the soil texture range – clay and sand – benefit from the same treatment, which is an application of organic matter. With sandy soils, however, any application seems to disappear almost the moment you turn back towards the compost heap. This is because sandy soils are open, well aerated and warm up quickly, which makes life very comfortable for the bacteria and microbes that quickly multiply and rapidly munch their way through any amount of organic matter. Any nutrients produced by this process are, unfortunately, leached fairly quickly through the porous soil that has no clay particles to hang on to them. Sandy soils are often acid because their free-draining and porous nature has allowed the calcium to be washed out of the soil.

Chalk

If you have ever driven along a new road that has been cut through chalk bedrock, you were probably amazed at the depth of the chalk. It can be hundreds of metres deep and it makes the thin layer of dark topsoil look very insignificant indeed.

The chalk, gleaming white when first exposed, is made up of the remains of microscopic calcareous algae, along with the shell debris from other creatures. Realizing that this great depth of sediment was built up on the bottom of the sea gives you an idea of the timescale involved – hundreds of thousands of years – in the formation of geological features.

For the gardener, chalk poses one or two problems. Very often the layer of topsoil is very thin, sometimes just a few centimetres, which is a despairing thought, although if you live in a valley, it is likely to be deeper where soil has

Plants for sandy soil

THESE PLANTS, WHICH ARE COLOURFUL AND EASY TO GROW, THRIVE IN DRY, SANDY SOIL.

Brachyglottis 'Sunshine'
Ceanothus
Crambe maritima
Cytisus
Eryngium maritimum
Genista lydia
Helianthemum (2)
Lotus hirsutus (5)
Lychnis coronaria
Perovskia atriplicifolia (1)
Salvia argentea
Santolina chamaecyparissus (3)
Spartium junceum (4)

been washed down over the years. But look at natural chalk woodland that is neither cultivated, grazed or unduly exposed, and you will see wild shrubs and trees growing to a good size. This is because, as is the way with all woodlands, there is a regular annual dressing of organic mulch from falling leaves each autumn, as well as the addition of more woody material from dead branches. The ground is not disturbed by cultivation or compacted by being trodden on or driven over, and so it has over time developed a nutritious layer of topsoil that feeds the roots and helps retain moisture.

It is the gardener's job to emulate this as much as possible. Chalk soils are often free draining and therefore very dry but that does not mean they can be treated with impunity. If they are worked or compacted when too wet, they can, because of their fine texture, behave like clay and become very sticky. Once in this condition they can take years to recover. Lay down planks of wood on chalky soil to spread your weight when you work in wet weather; this will reduce compaction. If you need to barrow across a border, use planks, even when conditions are good. Copy the woodland model by applying a generous yearly mulch of organic material. For the best results, new borders will need, and this is the bit that hurts, digging to two spades' depth. The deepest spade's depth, or spit, will usually need breaking up with a heavy duty fork or even a pick, and then some organic manure mixed in to provide a food source and good root run as deep down as possible. It is worth the effort because it is the only chance you get to improve the lower levels before you plant.

Chalk soils are always alkaline. The plants for alkaline soils listed on page 132 will also do well on chalk soils.

Opposite

1 *Perovskia atriplicifolia*
2 *Helianthemum*
3 *Santolina chamaecyparisus*
4 *Spartium junceum*
5 *Lotus hirsutus*

FEEDING THE SOIL

Different fertilizers are recommended for different purposes in the garden: one for roses, one for containers and one for vegetables. Each has a different formulation of chemicals but this is not usually shown on the package, so the contents remain a mystery. However, lawn fertilizers usually display an 'analysis' on the packet, giving a clue as to what's inside.

If you buy a bag of lawn fertilizer, you will see a set of three numbers marked on the packaging. If it is a spring and summer fertilizer, then the numbers are likely to be 20:10:10, and there may also be the letters N, P and K. These letters are the chemical symbols for the three important constituents of the fertilizer and the numbers represent the percentage of those constituents. So, in this case there is 20 per cent nitrogen (N), 10 per cent phosphorus (P) and 10 per cent potassium (K) in the fertilizer; the rest of the fertilizer will be a carrier.

Nitrogen is vital for plant growth because it is a crucial part of the green pigment chlorophyll that gathers light energy. It is important in spring and summer when the grass is growing most vigorously and has a high demand for nitrogen. But do not be tempted to apply more than the recommended rate: an overdose of nitrogen can lead to excessively lush growth, which not only means more lawn mowing but the grass will be more prone to disease and less resistant to wear and tear. An autumn lawn fertilizer will have a typical N:P:K ratio of 3:10:10 because grass needs far less nitrogen during the winter.

Phosphorus plays a vital part in seed germination and the development of the root system, and so is particularly important when establishing new lawns from seed, as well as encouraging a good root growth when the turf is laid. Potassium, meanwhile, is involved in various processes important to the well being of plants in general and not specifically to grass. It gives plants a toughness that helps them survive extreme conditions of cold and dry.

Both phosphorus and potassium get locked in the ground, but nitrogen is quickly leached through the soil by rain. For that reason, look for a controlled release fertilizer that drip-feeds small amounts of nitrogen over a long period. The notion that nutrients like phosphorus and potassium have very specific functions, such as root, fruit or flower production, is a little misleading. They are tied up with a range of functions within the plant and can cause different effects given different conditions. As long as they have an adequate and balanced supply of all the nutrients, the vast majority of plants will produce healthy leaves, flowers and fruit.

MULCHES, MANURES AND COMPOST HEAPS

It is beyond my understanding why more gardeners do not make use of mulches, if only for their very obvious weed-suppressing and, therefore, labour-saving qualities. Mulches are an important part of the recycling of energy and nutrients within the garden. With every leaf burnt and every bag of weeds carted to the tip there is a subtraction from the organic content of the garden.

The great quantities of leaves either burnt, stuffed into green bags or carted to the tip each autumn never ceases to amaze me. I suspect that much of the clearing away is done in the name of tidiness. Most leaves that fall on borders can be left, so long as they are not smothering plants; worms will pull them in. Large leaves like those of the fig, *Paulownia* and *Catalpa* are big enough to smother smaller plants, so should be removed. It is important to remove leaves from the lawn, otherwise the grass will be killed through lack of light, and their removal will discourage worm activity. They are ideally collected with a rotary lawn mower, which will not only shred them but also mix them up with grass cuttings to help in their decomposition.

Shredding any vegetation hastens the process of composting by rupturing cells and exposing a greater surface area of plant material to the microbes that do the breaking down. An example of the difference it makes was made obvious to me after I had scythed an area of long grass and piled the cut grass in a heap to decompose. Shortly afterwards I made another pile from grass cut with a mower.

The mown pile, where the stems were rent and smashed by the mower, started to heat up within an hour of being tipped, but the scythed pile, where the stems were intact, did not heat up at all. This was because the plants' undamaged natural barriers were keeping the bacteria at bay and slowing the decomposition process right down.

There can be a surprising amount of heat generated in a well-managed heap; it will become so hot, in fact, that you won't be able to put your hand into it. It is this heat that kills weed seeds in the compost heap, which is an important function. To think that all the heat energy is generated by the activity of microscopic organisms makes the process all the more astonishing.

Grass cuttings, provided they are treated properly, are an ideal ingredient for the compost heap. They provide moisture and an abundance of nitrogen. Microbes need nitrogen to generate their protein. Heaped on their own, grass cuttings heat up, then sink down into a smelly and slimy mess. This is because as they settle all the air is squashed out of the heap so that only anaerobic bacteria (those that need no oxygen) can function; it is these bacteria that produce the smell.

What is needed in the heap to prevent the smell and slime are air and carbon. The carbon is used by bacteria with the nitrogen to synthesize protein, and the air will provide oxygen for the odourless aerobic bacteria. The easiest way to provide both air and carbon is to combine the grass with straw in an approximately equal mix. Straw is mostly carbon but apart from supplying this element, it fluffs up the mix and its natural hollow structure allows air into the heap. Regular turning is recommended to maintain a well-aerated heap, but my experience has been that if there is sufficient straw in the mix and it is well tossed to start with, it will break down quite rapidly without further mixing. Although wood shavings will provide the necessary carbon, they are not as efficient as straw at keeping the heap open and aerated, so it will require more turning. Leaves are also a source of carbon, if nothing else is available. If you are shredding herbaceous stems and woody twigs, it is useful to throw fresh grass cuttings through the shredder as you go to get nitrogen into what is an overly woody, carbon-rich heap. The smaller the pieces of woody material you shred, the greater the access for bacteria. And the more nitrogen made available through green soft vegetation, the quicker the breakdown.

Tree and shrub leaves contain much more woody fibre than fleshy herbaceous leaves, such as grass, and take longer to break down. However, because they decompose more slowly, they offer a good source of long-term organic matter, which helps to retain moisture in the soil.

Proprietary compost accelerators are available and they are very effective. They usually comprise sulphate of ammonia with a bulking agent or carrier, although sulphate of ammonia can be bought more cheaply on its own. As the ammonia breaks down, nitrogen is freed to stimulate bacterial activity.

It is not advisable to dig uncomposted materials like straw and wood shaving into the soil because they are mostly carbon and as the bacteria feed on them they will deplete the soil of nitrogen. There is a converse side to this that comes into play if the land is not being planted for a few weeks. Once the bacteria have used up all their food source (straw, wood shavings and so on), they will die in their millions, releasing the nitrogen and carbon back into the soil and making it available to plants. The ideal solution with only partly decomposed material is not to dig it in but to apply it to the soil surface, where the interface between mulch and soil is minimal. Some nutrients will leach down but there will not be a great depletion of the nitrogen that is much needed by the plants.

Why add mulches?

Mulches have several benefits when applied thickly. They smother weed seedlings and prevent light from reaching the soil surface, thereby stopping many weed seeds from germinating. As they break down, mulches gradually release a steady stream of nutrients into the soil. They also encourage worm activity by offering food to the worm. The worm, in turn, aerates the soil and takes the organic matter down below the surface (see page 144 to find out just how much), which improves the soil's water-holding capacity. Mulches help prevent the soil surface from drying out by evaporation, and this helps reduce drought stress during the summer, as well as minimizing the cracking in clay soils. If you have to walk on the garden, a deep mulch will help spread your weight, meaning that you cause less compaction. An organic mulch also protects the surface from the pounding effect of rain, which can seal the surface with a compacted crust.

A final benefit is one of aesthetics. Stony soils can look very impoverished when the rain has washed the surface, leaving stones standing proud and catching the eye almost as much as the plants. An attractive mulch masks the surface, gives it a richer, healthier look and also darkens it so that the plants are shown off to their best.

It's a mistake to think that mulches will suppress perennial weeds. Thistles, nettles, docks and bindweed will not be checked in any way; regular mulching will result only in bigger, stronger and healthier perennial weeds, and more serious measures are needed to control them. That said, I have made life a little easier by heavily mulching a shrub border containing the pernicious ground elder for three successive years, to find that the ground elder became established in the top layer of mulch and soil and was much easier to dig out. Be warned, this will not work with bindweed!

SLUGS AND SNAILS

The soil is a rich medium teeming with life, from the tiniest bacteria – there are ten million nematodes per square metre in the top few centimetres of a healthy soil – to much larger creatures like slugs and worms. With plants being an integral part of soil life, it is not surprising that at least some of these soil dwellers have taken advantage of plants as a food source. In fact, what is surprising is that there are not more of them intent on eating plant material.

Slugs and snails (I have included snails here because they are similar to slugs in many ways, even though they live mainly on or near the soil surface) are two of the major pests to the gardener and possibly the least understood. By no means are all of them garden pests. Many slugs and snails eat dead and decaying plant material, fungi and dead animal matter. Some slugs are predatory and eat other slugs and earthworms.

They are a sexually mixed-up group. Most are hermaphrodite so, after an often elaborate courtship and mating, both partners are likely to lay eggs. Some species change from being male to female as they age and others fertilize themselves without having to find a mate. Slugs once had protective shells but now just one species has the visible vestige of one, while the others make the most of their shell-less form and work themselves well down into the soil in search of food. This, unfortunately, can mean plant roots, carrots, dahlia tubers and potatoes all suffer; research has even shown that if there is a choice, slugs have a preference for which potato variety they eat.

Some slugs are a nondescript grey like the seriously damaging field slug, but the large black, ridged and glistening *Arion ater* is something to behold and much less damaging than its size would suggest. Look out for *Arion distinctus* and its two close relatives *A. owenii* and *A. hortensis*, which have a bright orange sole. They are big and beautiful, don't you agree?

What to do about these creatures? There are almost as many tricks for getting rid of slugs and snails as there are types of slug. Most of them seem to be based on the assumption that snails and slugs do not like to walk over surfaces that we think would be uncomfortable. Having lived in an old house with damp walls and poorly fitting doors I have had first-hand experience of slugs. I have seen them walk over what I would have thought very irritating surfaces that could have been easily avoided with a simple detour. One particular creature, having made its way across a nice smooth stone floor, carried on in a straight line across dry, dusty grit that had come from the doormat, up and across the bristly and dry doormat, back on to the stone floor, then, apparently without a second thought, straight on to a very dry, bristly, woollen carpet for a long haul to the other end of the room. I thought that such a distance must surely have dried up its entire supply of slime, but it didn't. Who knows what was driving him on, but when he reached the foot of a cupboard he stopped.

Far left From the moment lupins come through the ground, snails consider their fleshy stems and leaves to be the tastiest morsels in the garden.

Below Pieces eaten out of leaves, stems chewed through and seedlings grazed to short stumps could all be the work of a range of pests, from mice to caterpillars. But the telltale slime trail tells you that the damage is caused by slugs or snails.

This made me think about how effective some of the regularly suggested remedies might be, so I arranged circles of crushed egg shells, dry sharp sand, wet sharp sand and a circle of dry soot on a board. I placed a couple of snails (I couldn't find any slugs at the time) in each circle to see what happened. Well, they all eventually just walked out of their circles except for those in the circle of soot, so perhaps dry soot is the answer – at least until it rains. Not very scientific, I know, but I suggest you forget all those remedies and rely on reducing the damage by reducing the population. This means trapping them by attracting them to upturned grapefruit skins, discarded cabbage leaves or the reliable beer trap – a shallow dish of beer sunk to ground level and refreshed every four or five days. Check your traps in the morning and drop your catch into very salty or very hot water. Don't throw them into your neighbour's garden! Removing slugs by hand leaves you with slime-covered fingers, and it is surprising how difficult it is to wash off.

Slugs need to be tempted from below ground but snails live above ground and can easily be collected at late evening or early morning, particularly during moist weather. Snails need calcium to build their shells, which means they are more likely to be a problem in areas with calcareous soils and naturally occurring sources of lime.

Dry stone walls provide ideal hiding places and good snail hunting grounds. Snails seal themselves up and sit out the winter in dark dry places and can often be found crowded together in considerable numbers under wooden shed floors, in the wood store and similar places. Winter is a good time to collect them, though you may feel rather heartless as you prise them from their rest.

There is a trade-off between keeping the garden clear of all organic debris including mulches, which will reduce the slug and snail population, and mulching to keep the soil fertile and moist and risk slug and snail damage. A small weight that might tip the balance in favour of mulching is that birds find it easier to scratch through loose and friable (crumbly) soil to find and eat the slugs and snails along with other soil pests.

EARTHWORMS

It is impossible when it comes to the fundamentals of gardening and the well-being of the soil not to give a special mention to the earthworm. The beneficial effects of this creature's behaviour are completely disproportionate to its size and visibility. Such is their impact that they give rise to wonderful statistics. For example, in an orchard the lob worm (*Lumbricus terrestris*), which can grow up to 30cm (1ft) in length, will remove 90 per cent of the leaf litter, which amounts to some 1.2 tonnes per hectare (1¼ tons per 2½ acres) – and that's dry weight. In a year they can also produce some 25,000 kg per hectare (24¼ tons per 2½ acres) of worm casts on the surface, which must go some way to explain why we have to dig down so far to find archaeological remains.

Worms come up out of the ground and drag leaves back down with them to digest in the safety of their holes. Although they do this in the open ground, it's more likely to happen between paving slabs or in gravel drives, where you may notice little tufts of half-buried leaves poking through.

Not all worms make their casts on the surface; some make them underground, filling cracks and crevices. From egg to adult takes 30–40 weeks, and while the lob worm can live for three or four years, other worms might survive only a few weeks as adults. Some live in the surface leaf litter, some just below this level in the soil and others as far as two metres (seven feet) down. Earthworms prefer an alkaline soil, which provides the calcium they need for their internal workings.

Earthworms are surprisingly good at getting through compacted soil because they eat their way through it rather than trying to squeeze through, and the soil that passes through them forms stable crumbs, which improve the soil structure.

Worms have no ears or eyes but are sensitive to light and have a keen sense of touch. They are able to discern which is the narrow end of a leaf and drag that end into their hole first, so that it will go in easier, and they discriminate in favour of leaves that are rich in nutrients over poorer and less palatable leaves.

In fertile established grassland there may be 500–700kg of earthworms per hectare (½–¾ ton per 2½ acres) but cultivating the ground can reduce that number by as much as 70 per cent, which is a very good argument for adopting the 'no dig' approach to gardening. Earthworms are also at risk from predators, such as birds, badgers, foxes and moles, and centipedes eat their eggs.

Lob worms stretch out of their burrows at night but leave their tail tight in the hole so that at the slightest threat they can instantly pull themselves back to safety. While stretched out they sweep leaves and small stones towards the hole.

One curious fact about worms is that they seem able to climb. I have found them a metre and a half (five feet) from the ground in moist debris in the fork of a tree, as well as slithering up a pane of glass that had been leaned against a wall.

Name that plant

Clearing up the confusion

You might think that life would be a lot easier if plants lost their complicated scientific names and had only simple common names, like Jack in the pulpit, lords and ladies and cuckoo pint. But you'd be wrong.

Top left *Crocus chrysanthus.* Crocus comes from *krokos,* Greek for saffron, and *chrysanthus* from the Greek *chrysos* meaning gold and *anthemon*, flower.

Top right *Clematis*, from the Greek *clema*, a tendril.

Bottom left *Gardenia augusta*, after the late 18th-century botanist Dr Alexander Garden and *augusta* from the Latin for dignified or noble.

Bottom right *Aster novi-belgii*, the New York aster, comes from the Greek *aster*, a star, and *novi-belgii*, an historic name for New York.

These particular common names all belong to the same plant, *Arum maculatum*, which shows just how important it is for plants to have a single scientific name, so that when we refer to them we can be sure that we are talking about the same plant. No matter where you are in the world, a plant's scientific name is the same; the common name, however, differs from country to country.

Many people seem unduly put off by the scientific names of plants, but they really are simpler to understand than you might imagine. You don't have to be a botanist or a classics scholar to have some grasp of how they work or, indeed, to get pleasure from them: seeing the links between names, discovering the historic stories behind them, relating names to the language we use today as well as seeing the names in a botanical context. Curiosity is all you need.

The most frequently asked questions about plant names is why do they sound so complicated, how on earth do you remember them all and why do they keep changing. The answers are all bound to each other.

How does anyone remember them? Well, first of all, you don't learn them all at once; you pick them up one or two at a time and they gradually accumulate in your memory. Using the names regularly is an important part of remembering. If you're wondering where to start, look at the following list. No matter how little experience you have as a gardener, you will surprise yourself as to how many scientific names you already know. *Lobelia, Fuchsia, Delphinium, Petunia, Begonia, Gardenia, Capsicum, Angelica, Philadelphus, Acer, Deutzia, Rhododendron, Hydrangea, Camellia, Berberis, Ribes, Forsythia, Mahonia, Pyracantha, Viburnum, Heuchera, Agapanthus, Aster, Bergenia* and *Iris* are all legitimate scientific names, and there are undoubtedly many more that you would recognize.

In a way similar to us, plants have a two-part name – one name ties them to close relatives, much as our surnames, and the other sets them apart as individuals. With plants, the surname, or genus, comes before the individual or species name, for example *Primula denticulata* and *Acer palmatum*.

UNDERSTANDING PLANT LABELS

It is probably in garden centres that you most often come across these botanical plant names, or at least part of them. Garden centres strive to make everything as easy as possible for the customers, and we all agree with that practice, but it can mean that they label their plants with the simplest form of the plant name, leaving out everything but the genus – the plant's surname – and the variety.

When you start to understand plant names, you will find this a very frustrating practice. It gives you no chance of working out what species the plant has come from, thereby getting some idea of its characteristics. An example is *Fuchsia magellanica* var. *molinae* 'Sharpitor', which is likely to be labelled simply as *Fuchsia* 'Sharpitor'. Good idea, do I hear you say? Tut, tut! No it's not. Had the word *magellanica* been included, those with a little plant knowledge would have known straight away that this is a hardy fuchsia. Those with a greater understanding would have known it is likely to have the almost white flowers associated with the variety *molinae*.

Let's take a common plant like *Pyracantha* and look at its name as it might appear on a garden centre label. Fortunately, its full name *Pyracantha rogersiana* 'Flava' is displayed. The first part, *Pyracantha*, is the name of the genus (the plural of genus is genera). This tells us that it belongs to a genus whose plants all have sufficiently similar botanical features to show that they are very closely related. The species of this plant is *rogersiana*, named in honour of G.L. Coltman-Rogers, who was the first to exhibit these young plants in 1913. Convention dictates that the genus is written in italics and starts with a capital letter. In *Pyracantha rogersiana* 'Flava', the second part of the name, *rogersiana*, is called the species. This always starts with a small letter and is written in italics.

Certain plants are the result of such complicated hybridizing and crossbreeding that their origins are unclear. Others are selections or hybrids that arose a very long time ago and no records exist of their true origin. With both these types of plant just the genus and cultivar name are quoted, as here with *Fuchsia* 'Madame Cornélissen', an almost hardy variety introduced in 1860.

The third part of the name 'Flava' is the cultivar. Cultivar is short for cultivated variety and denotes a plant that has arisen or been perpetuated in cultivation rather than in the wild. Cultivars – often called varieties, although this is not strictly correct – are written with a capital letter in roman, not italics, and enclosed in single quotation marks. So, 'Flava' indicates that the plant is a cultivar. Another flick through the dictionary will show you that words with similar beginnings, for example flavin and flavescent, have something to do with the colour yellow. This *Pyracantha* cultivar has yellow berries instead of the usual orange.

Since 1959 cultivar names have not been allowed to be Latinized and must have a so-called 'fancy' name, so if this *Pyracantha* was discovered now, it would have to carry a name such as 'Yellow Glow'. There are some Latin cultivar names

that have survived, though, including 'Nigra' (black), 'Alba' (white), 'Pendula' (pendulous), 'Laciniata' (cut-leaved), 'Atropurpurea' (purple), 'Fastigiata' (fastigiate, that is, upright), 'Argentea' (silver) and 'Nana' (small).

WHAT'S IN A NAME?

Many plant names are obvious in their connections and commemorate people who were important botanists or sponsors of plant-collecting trips. The genus *Buddleja*, for example, was named in honour of a Reverend Adam Buddle, while the species *Buddleja davidii* was named for the French missionary Armand David. His name is also commemorated in the pocket handkerchief tree *Davidia involucrata*. *Berberis wilsoniae*, meanwhile, was named for the wife of the renowned plant collector Ernest Wilson. If you know a little Latin, you'll realize that it's the feminine version of Wilson being used here.

With some plant names it is easy to jump to the wrong conclusion. A plant with the species name *australis* need not come from Australia, as this term simply means 'of the southern hemisphere'. *Helleborus orientalis* comes from no further afield than Greece and Turkey, which were considered quite eastern countries when this plant was named.

Other plant names are purely descriptive and are derived from Greek or Latin. Some describe the habit of the plant, so *Melianthus major* is the largest of the melianthuses and *Ceanothus prostratus* is a prostrate ground-hugging plant. Some names describe the flowers: *Digitalis grandiflora* has large flowers, *Digitalis parviflora*, small; *Althaea rosea*, pink; and *Magnolia stellata*, star-like. Other names describe the leaves: *Salvia microphylla* has small leaves, *Acer macrophyllum*,

large; *Buxus sempervirens*, evergreen (derived from *semper* meaning always and *virens* meaning green); and *Larix decidua*, deciduous. The name *Pyracantha* can be split into two parts: *pyr*, the Greek for fire (this is also the root of the word pyrotechnics) and *acanthus*, from the Greek for thorn. Put the two root words together and you get fire thorn, which is, as you probably know, the common name of the plant.

Some names simply describe where a plant comes from, and you would be right in thinking that *Euonymus europaeus* originates in Europe, but you would be wrong in assuming that *Cedrus atlantica* hails from the Atlantic. In fact, it comes from the Atlas Mountains of North Africa. Make no mistake about *Scilla peruviana* either – it comes from Spain! It seems that Linnaeus, the famous 18th-century Swedish botanist who began this system of giving plants Latin names, slipped up on this occasion, muddling the name of the boat 'The Peru' that brought it from Spain with the country of origin.

A hybrid between two species is marked by a cross and either given a name that combines the names of the two species or given a completely new name. This is the case with *Iris* x *robusta*, a hybrid between *Iris versicolor* and *Iris virginica*.

FATHOMING HYBRIDS

The names of hybrids are more complicated to fathom, so let's start with a pretty straightforward one: *Lonicera* x *brownii* 'Dropmore Scarlet'. This honeysuckle, with heads of bright red tubular flowers is a hybrid between *Lonicera sempervirens* and *Lonicera hirsuta*. Not all species within a genus are necessarily able to interbreed but some can and this one did. The resultant hybrid sometimes has the best attributes of both plants and is therefore superior to either of its parents. This can be useful, for example, when you are able to cross a slightly tender species that has showy flowers with a hardy but less beautiful species and the hybrid inherits the hardiness and the large flowers. The hybrid is given a new specific name, but to denote that it is a hybrid and not a true species an 'x' is put before that name, hence *Lonicera* x *brownii*. As mentioned earlier, the name in quotation marks is the cultivar, in this case 'Dropmore Scarlet', a plant raised by a Mr Skinner from Dropmore in Canada.

The genetic difference between two genera is greater than the difference between two species within a genus and therefore it is much more unusual to produce hybrids between them. However, it does happen occasionally and in the case of X *Sophrolaeliocattleya* the hybrid is between three genera of orchid: *Sophronitis, Laelia* and *Cattleya*. Many of the orchid hybrids are artificially generated by specialist breeders. The X before the generic name lets us know that it is a generic hybrid.

We now go from one extreme – the highly specialized world of the orchid breeder – to another: garden hedging. X *Cupressocyparis leylandii* is the overused, often mismanaged and both despised and cherished Leylandii hedging. This fast-growing tree is the result of a hybrid between two conifers, and the cross before the name tells us that the hybrid was created from two different genera: *Cupressus* and *Chamaecyparis*. The former gives the hybrid its vigour and drought-tolerance, the latter its hardiness. The original plants occurred as seedlings near Welshpool in Wales in the grounds of a Mr Naylor's estate. They were taken to Northumberland and planted in the property of a Mr Leyland in the early 1890s.

'Why do they keep changing plant names?' is a commonly heard complaint when plants we have known for years suddenly become something else. *Datura*, for example, became unfamiliar *Brugmansia*. But look back far enough and you will see that the plant was originally called *Brugmansia*, and the rules say that this name must take precedence. No doubt people were upset originally when it became *Datura*.

Much more formidable-looking and, admittedly, an exceptional example of a scientific name is X *Cupressocyparis leylandii* (Dallim. & A.B.Jackson) Dallim. 'Robinsons Gold'. I hope I have already gone some way to making this name more accessible. We now understand why there is an X; we know that Mr Leyland gave his name to the new hybrid; and we know that the cultivar name 'Robinsons Gold' was selected for some special characteristic. In this case, it was the foliage, which goes from bronze through to gold as the season progresses.

That just leaves the names inside and in front of the brackets. These relate to the people who gave authority to the plant name. For this hybrid it was Messrs Dallimore and Jackson, who studied the plant and traced its parentage, gave it the name *Cupressus* x *leylandii* and published a description. Further research and the splitting of the genus Cupressus by botanists caused it to be renamed as we know it today. The brackets enclose the original authority, and this is followed by a reference to a more recent authority, Dallimore, outside the brackets (this is, in fact, the same Dallimore, who reclassified the plant).

ALL CHANGE

The species name separates the genus into plants that have characteristics that make them different from other plants in that genus, but not sufficiently different to warrant their own genus. These differences have occupied botanists for many decades, and some plants have been in and out of different genera as various opinions have held sway. Where the differences are even smaller, arguments have arisen as to whether a plant deserves its own status as a species or is simply a minor variation of an existing species.

Disputes over which genus plants belong to usually affect only a tiny minority of plants and are possibly sparked by a botanist finding some detail of a plant's structure that means its classification needs to be reassessed. Now and then, however, they lead to some major name changes. It is when the names of plants you have known for a long time are changed that the system, as proper as it might be, becomes frustrating. A good example of this was when a whole range of plants, *Chrysanthemum*, was broken down into *Leucanthemum*, *Argyranthemum* and a long list of other 'themums' and genera.

You may come across a plant name followed by 'syn.' and then by another plant name. Syn. stands for synonym, and it is used to refer to the name by which the plant was previously known, for example *Leucanthemum vulgare* syn. *Chrysanthemum leucanthemum*.

saprophytes 95
saxifrages 40
scents 66, 112, 115
scientific names 148–54
scrophularia weevils 92
Sedum telephium 39–40
seed pods 108
seedlings, genetic diversity 116
seeds 120–5, *122*, *123*, *125*
self-defence 30–3
self-fertilization 116–19
Sempervivum *27*, 40, 94
sepals *108*
Sequoia sempervirens 23
Sequoiadendron giganteum 23
sex, dioecious plants 111–12
shade-tolerant plants 16
shredders 140, 141
shrubs: roots 49
  wall shrubs 70, 76
  woody stems 18–19
signals, chemical 87–8
silty soil 133–4
Silybum marianum 63, *64*
sloping sites 42–3
slugs 99, 102, 143–4
snails 99, 119, 143–4, *143*
soap, insecticidal 101
soil 128–45
  capping 135–7
  chalky soil 128, 137–9
  clay soil 128, 133–4, 135–7, *136*, 142
  drainage 135, 137
  earthworms 144–5
  fertilizers 139–40
  and flower colour 60
  mulches 140, 142, 144
  pH values 130–3
  roots 52
  sandy soil 133–4, 137, *138*
  structure 134–5
  testing 130, 133–4
  texture 133–4
solanine 85
Solanum melongena 31
X *Sophrolaeliocattleya* 153
spadix 118
Spartium junceum 138
spathes 118, 119
species: hybrids 153
  names 148, 150, 154
spines 30–2, *30–3*, 81
spores, fungal diseases 95, 96
'sports' *65*
stamens 106
standard trees 19
Stapelia 66
Stellaria media 116
stems 16–29
  bark 20–4
  growing tips 17–18
  herbaceous stems 18
  shapes 19–20
  woody stems 18–19
stigmas 108, *108*, *109*, 111, 114, 117, 119, 120
stolons 26–7
stomata 13–14, 38, 52
stony soils 142
straw 141, 142
strawberries 26, *26*
styles 108–9, *109*, 115, 117
succulents 38, 40–1
sulphur 133
sunflowers 115, *121*
supports, climbers 72, 73
sweet peas 73, 119
sweetcorn 109
sycamore 122
synonyms, plant names 154
systemic pesticides 98–9
systemic weedkillers 103

T

Tanacetum cinerariifolium 83
tannin 84
taproots 48
Taxus 111
  T. baccata 82
temperature: adaptation to 40, 44–5
  compost heaps 141
  and germination 120, 121
tender plants 41
tendrils, climbers 72–4, *72*, *74–5*
Teucrium 19
thistles 31, 32, 103, 142
thorns 30–1, *32*, 74–7, *76–7*
thrum-eyed flowers 119
ties 24
Tolmiea menziesii 15
tomatoes 85, 87
topsoil 128–30, 137–9
toxic chemicals 82, 83–7
training stems 17, *17*
trees: bark 20–4, *22*, *23*
  defence chemicals 86
  growth rings 20–2
  microclimates 42
  pollen 111
  roots 49
  standard trees 19
  in winter 44–5
  woody stems 18–19
Tropaeolum 'Alaska' 65
  T. speciosum 73
  T. tuberosum 29, 73
tubers 28–9
tulips 96, *97*, 106
twining plants 70–2

U

ultraviolet light 58, *60*, 113–14
Urtica dioica 111

V

variegated leaves 63–5, *63–5*
vegetables 48, 96
veins, leaves *11*, 12–13, *13*
Viburnum 113, 120
  V. opulus 15, 90, *132*
Vinca major 136
  V. minor 48
vine weevils *92–3*, 93–4, 99, 100
Viola 125
  V. odorata 116, *116*
viral markings, variegated plants 65
virus diseases 96–8, *96*, *97*
Vitis vinifera 72–3

W

Waldsteinia ternata 26–7
wall shrubs 70, 76
walls, microclimates 41–2
wasps, gall 95
water: in clay soil 135
  drought-tolerant plants 36–41
  photosynthesis 12
  roots and 49–52
  transport in stems 18
water lilies 13–14
watering 49–50
waterlogging 52
weedkillers 102–3
weeds: mulches 142
  rhizomes 25–6
  roots 48
  seed dispersal 125
  self-fertilization 116
weevils 91–4
wheat 50, 98
white flowers 61
whitefly 100
willow 62, 87, 94, 95, 98, 111, 122
willowherb 122, *122*
Wilson, Ernest 151
wind: and climbers 77
  seed dispersal 122–3, *122*, *123*
  wind-pollinated flowers 111–12
Wisteria 19, 70, 72
witches brooms 94
woodworm 91
woody stems 18–19
worms 140, 142, 143, 144–5, *145*

X

xylem cells 18, 19, 20, 52

Y

yew 82, 111
Yucca 36, 82, *82*

Acknowledgments

Author's acknowledgments

Special thanks to all the team at Conran Octopus for their help, encouragement and tolerance; they were a pleasure to work with. Thanks also to David Lamb for the book title.

Publisher's acknowledgments

The publisher would like to thank the following photographers and agencies for their kind permission to reproduce the photographs in this book:

1 Vaughan Fleming/The Garden Picture Library; 2 Jerry Harpur/Harpur Garden Library; 2–3 Rex Butcher/The Garden Picture Library; 4 above Andrew Lawson; 4 below Deni Bown/Oxford Scientific Films; 5 above left Andrew Lawson; 5 above right Mark Bolton; 5 below left Andrew Lawson; 5 below right Steffen Hauser/Oxford Scientific Films; 6–7 Francois De Heel/The Garden Picture Library; 8–9 Jerry Harpur/Harpur Garden Library; 11 Andrea Jones; 13 above Andrea Jones; 13 below Andrea Jones; 14 Mark Bolton; 15 David G. Fox/Oxford Scientific Films; 17 Clive Nichols; 18 Marianne Majerus; 19 Mark Bolton/The Garden Picture Library; 21–3 Andrew Lawson; 25 Andrea Jones; 26 Jerry Harpur/Harpur Garden Library; 27 Christi Carter/The Garden Picture Library; 29 Mel Watson/The Garden Picture Library; 30–1 S & O Mathews Photography; 32 left Michelle Lamontagne/The Garden Picture Library; 32 right Marianne Majerus; 33 left Mark Bolton; 33 right Mark Bolton/The Garden Picture Library; 34–5 Nigel Francis/The Garden Picture Library; 36 Marcus Harpur/Harpur Garden Library; 37 Marianne Majerus; 39 Andrew Lawson; 40 Marianne Majerus; 43 S & O Mathews Photography; 45 Howard Rice/The Garden Picture Library; 46–7 Marianne Majerus; 48 Clive Nichols; 49 Joy Michaud/Flower Photos; 51 Jerry Pavia/The Garden Picture Library; 53 above left Clive Nichols; 53 below left Marcus Harpur/Harpur Garden Library; 53 right Andrew Lawson; 54 John Glover/The Garden Picture Library; 55 Jerry Harpur/Harpur Garden Library; 56–7 Dave Tully/Flower Photos; 59 Andrew Lawson; 60 Owen Newman/Oxford Scientific Films; 61 Jerry Harpur/Harpur Garden Library; 62 Marcus Harpur/Harpur Garden Library; 63 Clive Nichols; 64 Andrea Jones; 65 S & O Mathews Photography; 66 Clive Nichols; 67 above left Marianne Majerus; 67 above right John Glover/The Garden Picture Library; 67 below Clive Nichols; 68–9 Jane Birdsell; 71 Clive Nichols; 72–3 Emma Peios/The Garden Picture Library; 73 Marcus Harpur/Harpur Garden Library; 74–5 Paul Williams; 76–7 S & O Mathews Photography; 78–9 Stephen Dalton/Natural History Photographic Agency; 80–1 Sunniva Harte/The Garden Picture Library; 82 left Andrew Lawson; 82 right Marcus Harpur/Harpur Garden Library; 83 Clive Nichols; 85 left Marianne Majerus; 85 right Andrea Jones; 87 David Cavagnaro/The Garden Picture Library; 89 Science Pictures Limited/Oxford Scientific Films; 91 above Andrea Jones; 91 below Clive Nichols; 92–3 Vaughan Fleming/The Garden Picture Library; 95 Howard Rice/The Garden Picture Library; 96 JS Sira/The Garden Picture Library; 97 Clive Nichols; 99 JS Sira/The Garden Picture Library; 100 N. A. Callow/Natural History Photographic Agency; 101 Stephen Dalton/Natural History Photographic Agency; 102 Stephen Dalton/Natural History Photographic Agency; 103 Bjorn Forsberg/The Garden Picture Library; 104–5 Marcus Harpur/Harpur Garden Library; 107 Sunniva Harte/The Garden Picture Library; 108 left Andrea Jones; 108 right Chris Burrows/The Garden Picture Library; 109 John Glover/The Garden Picture Library; 110 Howard Rice/The Garden Picture Library; 111 Steven Wooster/The Garden Picture Library; 113 Bjorn Forsberg/The Garden Picture Library; 114 John Ferro Sims/The Garden Picture Library; 115 Mark Bolton/The Garden Picture Library; 116 Marcus Harpur/Harpur Garden Library; 117 left Mark Bolton/The Garden Picture Library; 117 right Clive Nichols; 118–21 John Glover/The Garden Picture Library; 122 Jane Birdsell; 123 Mark Bolton; 125 Juliette Wade/The Garden Picture Library; 126–7 David Woodfall/Natural History Photographic Agency; 128 Bill Coster/Natural History Photographic Agency; 129 David Woodfall/Natural History Photographic Agency; 131 a Andrea Jones; 131 b Andrea Jones; 131 c Andrea Jones; 131 d Andrew Lawson; 132 a Andrew Lawson; 132 b Andrea Jones; 132 c Andrew Lawson; 132 d Clive Nichols (Eastgrove Cottage); 136 a Andrew Lawson; 136 b Andrea Jones; 136 c Andrew Lawson; 136 d Marianne Majerus; 136 e Andrea Jones; 136 f Marianne Majerus; 138 a, b & c Andrea Jones; 138 d Clive Nichols; 138 e Marianne Majerus; 141 Mark Bolton; 142 Jane Birdsell; 143 Mark Bolton/The Garden Picture Library; 145 David Thompson/Oxford Scientific Films; 146–7 Marcus Harpur/Harpur Garden Library; 149 above left James Guilliam/The Garden Picture Library; 149 above right Mark Bolton/The Garden Picture Library; 149 below left Clive Nichols; 149 below right Andrea Jones; 150 Clive Nichols; 151 Andrea Jones; 152 Mark Bolton/The Garden Picture Library; 155 Howard Rice/The Garden Picture Library

Every effort has been made to trace the copyright holders and we apologize in advance for any unintentional omissions, and would be pleased to insert the appropriate acknowledgment in any subsequent publication.

The publisher would also like to thank Sharon Amos and Hilary Bird.